D1706802

Hit the Road!

A Badass Mom's Guide for Families Who Want to Travel the World

by Zélie Pollon

Table Of Contents

Acknowledgements
Dream
Introduction

1. The Way Life Sometimes Plays Out 1
Lori Greene – Putting One Foot in Front of The Other 9

2. Face Your Fears 13
Jacqui and Daniel New –
Overcoming Fear to Take the First Step 18

3. Attitude is Everything 24
Alicia E. – Embracing Simplicity for a Calmer Life 30

4. Assessing Your Life, a Journaling Exercise 33
Rebecca Eichler and Paul Carlino –
Reinventing Yourself on the Road 37

5. The Time is Now 46
Cindy B. – Give Yourself Permission 50

6. Set Your Priorities 55
Allison Sherman –
The Schengen Zone and other Visa Restrictions 59

7. Build Your Community 67
Karen and Cameron King –
Mixing Full Time Travel and Work 71

8.   Where Should We Go? 78

Zoe McAdams –
   Finding Comfort and Safety Abroad 86

9.   Make a Plan for Your Stuff................................. 93

10. Get Your Documents in Order 100

Launch

11. What Happens When We Get There?................. 111

Jesica Sweedler Dehart –
   WWOOfing through Europe............................ 120

12. Slow Down.. 130

Jay Shapiro – Challenging What is "Normal"........ 133

13. Locate Your Tribe... 141

Lydia Bradbury – Military Families 147

14. Yes, there are Challenges
     when Traveling with Kids 153

15. Technology on the Road 161

Tony and Jade Burke – The Art of Deschooling 166

Learn

16. Schooling on the Road 173

Jennifer Sutherland Miller –
   Rethinking How Kids Learn............................ 181

17. Single Parent or Solo Travel 190
Caroline – The Logistical Rubik's Cube 202

18. Wellness and Health Care on the Road........... 209
Pati and Andrew Goodell –
   Choosing Opportunity When It Presents Itself......215

19. Travel Insurance 218
Aldis Barketis –
   The 411 on Expat and Traveler Insurance...... 224

Money
20. Financing Your Travel/Jobs on the Road........ 232
Tracey, Rob and Makai Tullis –
   In Search of a Family-Friendly Culture 257

21. Some Necessities for Remote Working 263
Chanel Morales – Take it Online!........................... 265

Paul Carlino –
   Don't Forget your Taxes!
   (Because your taxes will never forget you) 274

Connect
22. Travel Smarter...280
Astrid Vinji and Clint Bush –
   Making Travel Inclusive 287

23. Relationships...297

Shimea Hooks – Two-Mom Travel *303*

24. Are You Ready? A Journaling Exercise 308

Sandra Odems – Sail Those Seas! 310

25. Friendships..312

Lainie Liberti and Miro Siegel –
    Helping Worldschooling Teens and Adults to
    Find Their Way 319*

26. You Have Permission 331

Epilogue 334

Alicia Cardenas 337

INDEX 350
ABOUT THE AUTHOR 366

Acknowledgements

I'd like to thank all of the families I met on the road, who inspired this book and educated me along my own journey of traveling and parenting. I am forever grateful for the lessons and the friendships. I'd like to thank those who read early versions of the book, including Anna Goldstein, Patrick Lambert, Jesica Sweedler De-Hart, and Dr. Kate Green. Janine Pearson also gave invaluable feedback. Immense gratitude goes to my fabulous friend and editor Mary-Charlotte Domandi who was able to reflect back to me so many areas of this lifestyle that I sometimes take for granted. Her feedback made this a much better book. Designer Igacio Galván created a beautiful cover.

I dedicate this book to my greatest love and travel partner of all time, my son Aiden. It has been amazing to see the world through his eyes, to watch him grow and stretch through our various travels, and to now see such a capable and resourceful young man who continues to guide me on our journeys. This life of adventures has been my gift to you. I love you to the moon and back.

"Travel isn't always pretty. It isn't always comfort-able. Sometimes it hurts, it even breaks your heart. But that's OK. The journey changes you; it should change you. It leaves marks on your memory, on your consciousness, on your heart, and on your body. You take something with you. Hopefully, you leave some-thing good behind."

— Anthony Bourdain

Introduction

I wrote this book to inspire families who want to travel. It might even inspire some of you to move abroad indefinitely. Many of the families interviewed in this book decided to do just that. I have seen first-hand the incredible growth and learning that travel instills in people. It pushes us and makes us grapple with discomfort. It forces us to be flexible and patient, and sometimes out of control. It has exposed me to the immense natural beauty of this planet, and made me value the incredible diversity of the outdoors.

Those of us who have incorporated travel into our lives have seen the profoundly positive effects it has had on our children, and on their education. Travel necessarily opens your mind and pushes you to be vulnerable. It forces you to look at people and ways of living that are entirely different from your own. It gets you out of your comfort zone. This is how we grow in compassion, patience, and resilience. It's how we build peace with our neighbors.

Travel also helps us see more possibilities, even if we choose not to take them. The truth is that changing your environment can help change your mind, and changing your mind can help change your environment. But first you have to allow yourself to, and prepare for, change. If you once saw your path as set, this book will help show you that there are always opportunities to change course. The potential can be so much greater than you ever imagined. Plus, it can be so wonderfully fun.

Let this book become a door for you, inspiring you to think differently. What if travel were not a short-term escape, but an integral tool in your life? Travel can show you different ways of living, working, and teaching your children. It can suggest different modes of education and a step off the hamster wheel of how we define a proper life, job, and retirement. This book shows you there is no one way.

If you dream of travel for yourself and your family, let this be your blueprint — by which I mean a blueprint for your heart and your traveling soul. Let it inspire you and teach you, embolden you and connect you to others. You will find that there is any number of different and creative ways to build travel into your life. People are doing it every day, on every continent, and with all kinds of family and financial configurations. I share many of their stories and strategies in this book.

While there are similarities among the stories in these chapters, each family has chosen to do it differently. The one thing they share is a strong desire and creative mindset to make things happen. I hope their experiences inspire and inform you. Their stories might not answer *all* of your questions, but I hope they will bring your questions down to a digestible size and allow you to reframe your priorities.

I wrote these pages with a deep concern about sustainability in these dangerous times, and it's important to acknowledge that there is a carbon footprint to travel, and an even greater one from tourism. I make this distinction because I see tourism as a consumptive way to see the world, living outside a culture and looking in. For example, those all-inclusive resorts where you rarely interact with the people and place you are visiting? That's not the kind of adventure I'm talking about. Rather, this book seeks to inspire thoughtful and aware travel that has a light footprint and also teaches people to spend their dollars in ways that supports local communities. I want you to take a deeper dive and immerse yourselves in cultures with education in mind, and with a goal to give at least as much as you take. Because I believe that the impact of *not* traveling, *not* looking outside ourselves for bigger experiences different from those we already know — especially for young people — feels even more dangerous. I offer this guide as an antidote to hatred and bigotry, and a means to help heal divisions and create bridges.

Travel is not for everyone, and certainly not for all families. It is a luxury and a privilege, and with that comes responsibility. Americans in particular have the benefit of a US passport, which allows us easy access to most countries in the world. Similarly, an EU passport allows people to travel freely throughout the world. This isn't just about having resources and governmental allowance to cross borders, but also a mindset. People with these passports have the benefit of feeling free to travel, to see possibilities, to be brave enough to buck traditional education and modes of employment. This, too, is no small thing. Many people in the world have no such freedom.

Yet we still don't give ourselves permission.

These pages will address some common questions and offer travel hacks, including location, budget, strategies for lodging, education, general support and more. After each interview, families also have shared their favorite travel items, that have made their journeys easier. However, I've refrained from giving too many specific recommendations, as details change weekly and new and better resources become available every day. Rather, I want you to know where to look and how to connect with those already on the road.

This is more than a travel book. These pages are meant to encourage you to take a leap of faith in your life, whether for an extended trip or a move abroad. They are meant to remind you that life is short and you'd better get busy doing what you want — especially when you have kids. Time with children goes by fast, and the day when they walk out the door to live their own lives sneaks up with lightning speed. This book is telling you not to wait. Here's your roadmap, let's go!

Some Definitions

Before we begin, there are some educational terms that come up throughout this book and deserve a brief explanation. In practice, each of these educational methods may vary.

Traditional Schooling – includes both public and private schooling, and is based on a teacher-centered delivery method where a child often sits in a classroom to receive an education.

Homeschooling – is education generally given by parents to their children in a home setting. Sometimes this includes using traditional curriculum.

Unschooling – sometimes called "nature schooling" is informal learning led by the child as they live their daily life. There is no formal academic structure. A child learns by following their own interests.

Worldschooling – offers a child the opportunity to learn from the world. For families who are able, this often involves travel as a means of exposing children to places, people, and the sites of historical events as educational tools.

Deschooling – sometimes called unlearning, is the process that a child AND a parent go through after the student has left a traditional school setting to begin a different approach to learning, including the methods mentioned above. This adjustment period can take months before a new process of learning takes hold.

Chapter 1

The Way Life Sometimes Plays Out

2016 was a terrible year for me. Really terrible. It began with my mother's unexpected death from a brain aneurism. Then came the discovery of mold in my house, followed by thousands of dollars of mold remediation. I discovered black spots on my son's head that we thought for weeks might be sarcoma. Then I filed a restraining order against a colleague who threatened to kill me, followed by a minor surgery that skyrocketed into the tens of thousands of dollars. And that's just the Cliffs Notes.

When I finally left the country, I joked that I was escaping from my reality, because it was the only thing I had the strength left to do. The truth is that I had wanted to travel with my son – in fact spend more time with him in general – for years. I had taken on a more than full-time job running a radio station news department and I wanted to give it my all. It was new, exciting, challenging and rewarding in many ways. Plus, after years of freelance work, my mom was happy that I finally had a full-time job, and she let me know it repeatedly. Yet news reporting is never on a 9-5 schedule and the work eventually started killing me from the inside out. It's one thing if you justify a miserable job due to golden handcuffs; it's another entirely if you still can't pay the bills, you're in a constant state of stress and alert, and you haven't spent quality time with your child in weeks. I realized that I needed to rewrite the script. Fast. So we fled.

Now, you shouldn't have to lose a loved one or deal with a grave illness to reassess your life. You shouldn't have to be ground to a pulp to realize you can do better, that in fact you *must* do better. Yet that's often how it works. Extreme life events upend our lives, forcing us to overcome our fear of change. We have to hit bottom before we can even contemplate the life we really want.

Here's how my own story played out. The year was unfolding as I described above, and I was juggling the stresses and responsibilities with the skill of the multitasking single mom ninja that I am. I felt like a professional circus act with 20 extra balls thrown in the loop: the burial services, memorial, paperwork, and dealing with a home filled with my mother's belongings. I had to deal with her debts, her land, her friends and family. She had no actual cash to help lighten this load, so the stress reverberated. And that death threat from my co-worker? I had to fire him, which then doubled my own workload. Then, adding insult to injury, the station administration threw me under the bus.

One day in the middle of this Year from Hell, a dear friend asked me: "How is Aiden doing?" It wasn't just any question, but a heartfelt desire to know how my then nine-year-old son was dealing with the loss of his grandmother, with whom he had been very close.

It was a simple question, and one I should have been able to answer right away. I had some instant flashes: that I should have followed through with the grief counseling I had looked into, that I should have taken those days off with him to really sit and discuss this loss. I hadn't done any of that because I was waiting for a later date when I would have more time and feel more calm. That date didn't come. There was always more to do, more papers to sign, more people needing to see me, more meetings to schedule. The reality was that I had no idea how my son was dealing with the loss of his grandmother because all of my time and energy was being taken up in efforts to merely get by.

In that brief but profound moment I realized that I had to change course. I needed time to myself, and I needed to be less financially stressed. That meant I needed a lower cost of living in a place with a more relaxed pace of life. I needed to leave the US to create the time, space and clarity to ask the question and hear the answer: Aiden, how are you feeling?

Six months later my son and I were on a plane heading south of the border. Not everything fell into place right away, or the way I had initially hoped, but there were enough pieces of the puzzle that I could make our departure a reality.

As I look back, the most important factors that opened the doors to our first journey were a determined will, an ability to face fear, and a spirit of adventure – characteristics that luckily I had in spades. I'm not downplaying the other vital factors, like finances, but all of them were secondary to simply making the decision to change my life. Overcoming my fears – of the unknown, of a lack of stability, of a loss of control – or at the very least facing them, is the step that allowed the rest of the path to unfold.

A funny thing happened when I became clear on my plans: Once I told friends we were leaving, they thought it was a great idea. More people than I can count professed to me their regrets at not having traveled with their children when they could or "should" have. They shared how they dreamed of doing this or that but it never quite worked out. There wasn't the time or the money. Life got in the way. They shared these regrets as if a light bulb were suddenly turned on, as if my upcoming departure were releasing their forgotten possibilities and latent desires. I had had a similar experience in my early 30s when I traveled with my boyfriend at the time from New Mexico to Venezuela, the two of us atop his F650 BMW motorcycle. We were a good-looking pair, clad in leather, wind-worn faces and bright smiles. I imagined we looked the part of someone's lost hero journey. I say this because so many travelers (primarily male) we encountered along the way mused about how lucky we were, and how they'd always wanted to do something similar, but relationships, jobs, kids, and other responsibilities hadn't made it possible.

The look in these people's eyes, the depth of longing and regret I felt from perfect strangers as they watched us ride by, made a strong impression on me. Here were grown men spontaneously sharing their intimate and unmanifested desires. I had never heard anything like it. I knew I didn't want to be like them, sharing profound regrets with strangers twenty years down the road, and I knew even then that if I had waited too long, I might never have embarked on some of my own adventures, or made some of my biggest decisions.

I had always traveled, but that motorcycle trip reinforced my desire for a life of adventure. Whenever I got the chance, I would explore new countries and seek out fresh experiences. It has been an extraordinary life. As I grow older my travels change: I go slower and explore deeper. I always return with renewed perspective and an appreciation for everything I have, plus a critical eye for how my home country could do better. I am always filled with gratitude that I still have the health and energy to see this vast world.

In case you're wondering what happened with that crazy motorcycle love story: It started sputtering in Bolivia, hit major potholes in Colombia, and was extinguished for good once my partner (now solo) reached Argentina. Such adventures are opportunities for growth and self-reflection as much as they are for the journey itself. Sometimes that means growing apart.

The critical lesson of that voyage was that if you wait for life's circumstances to be perfect before taking an adventure that calls to you, it may never happen. I don't say this lightly. If there is something you really, truly want to do, then you must find a way to make it happen. Likewise, the decision to have a child is a parallel metaphor for the kind of travel this book invites. If you wait for every detail to fall into place, or for your finances to be perfect, you would never, and I mean *never*, have children.

Let this book help you take the first step.

Someone walking the beach asked if she could take
a picture of me and my son in Puerto Escondido, Mexico.

Lori Greene

Putting One Foot in Front of The Other

"If I can just survive until my kids go to college, I think I'll be ok."

Lori's story is similar to so many I heard from working parents living in the United States. Even with two parents working full time — she with a manufacturing company and her husband an engineer — the stresses of raising three kids in North America began taking a toll.

"I was so stressed out trying to manage everything in our lives, and mostly just the normal stuff that the majority of families in the US are dealing with. One day I thought, 'If I can just survive until my kids go to college, I think I'll be ok.'"

When she realized what she had just said, it seemed a terrible way to live. It inspired her to begin thinking about how to enjoy her life and her family more. On a vacation to Mexico, she fell in love with the town of San Miguel de Allende, and wanted to stay longer.

"We originally planned to be here a year, but I always wondered how we would be able to go back to the US after experiencing a year away. Within about a month of arriving in Mexico, we decided to stay indefinitely."

Lori had worked for the same company since 1994, and she was fortunate they agreed to let her work from Mexico. She already worked remotely, so now she was just "a little more remote," she said. In Mexico, her salary was enough to support the whole family.

They faced small challenges along the way, such as not knowing how or where to do things that were familiar in the US, like registering their car, getting a Mexican driver's license, or learning Spanish. In time, a less stressful and harried life with more time for her kids and husband far outweighed any challenge. Her kids attended small bilingual and international schools, participated in sports and volunteered with local organizations. They learned "empathy and compassion, social responsibility, flexibility, and curiosity about what's happening around them."

Lori's advice for others is not to let the logistical and emotional difficulties of a big move dissuade you.

"At some point in the planning and moving phase, most people feel overwhelmed and start to question whether they're doing the right thing. It doesn't help that friends and family in the US may not be supportive, or may express concern about safety and security."

Lori says to just keep moving forward and put one foot in front of the other. "Emptying our house in the US and purging decades of belongings was very hard for me. I felt like I hit a wall. I was anxious and worried. Then each morning I would wake up feeling re-energized. I'm glad I didn't cave in to the despair. That's what I tell other people who might be feeling the same: don't cave into the despair. A better life is around the corner."

Essential Travel Items

I can't live without my phone, so I always have a spare battery.

I also can't live without lip balm, and I have a fear of somebody getting sick or needing something, so I have a first aid kit and extras of all medicines.

I have a nice leather passport wallet that keeps everything organized, and a smallish backpack with lots of pockets.

I absolutely love Yeti products. I have several water bottles, a tumbler, a wine cup, and a cooler.

Chapter 2

Face Your Fears

My son and I were traveling through Ecuador as part of a nine-month exploration of Mexico and South America. One day, on a trip deep into the Ecuadorian side of the Amazon jungle I decided to face my incredible fear of heights. As it happened, facing fears was a common occurrence on this trip. This particular terror took the form of a crazy rope swing that hung from a tree that towered seemingly a thousand feet above the curves of the Amazon River as it snaked through the lush valley below. The arc of this swing was as wide as I'd ever seen, extending out over the valley for what felt like minutes. Tourists clung to the rope, often expelling a single, high-pitched scream throughout the entire arc. I watched, mesmerized, my palms sweating. 'I can do that' I repeated to myself, as I watched from the sidelines. In fact, I *must* do that. Suddenly it was as if my very belief in myself depended on it.

I hitched up my harness and wrapped my shaking legs around the wooden seat, which was attached to the end of the rope. The jungle guide held my harness to keep me from slipping off the platform. When the last safety buckle was clipped, he looked me in the eye as if to ask 'are you ready?' But he didn't wait for any response; he just pushed me off the cliff into the endless sky and sent me swinging out over the valley floor. When I finally could open my eyes and stop screaming, it was as if time had stopped. There I was with a cool fresh breeze in my face, suspended over the most beautiful scenery of my life: green, lush, fertile, and forgiving. How could I possibly have had so much fear about something so beautiful and exhilarating?

I couldn't initially see the beauty. I only saw through my perspective of fear. There were a million reasons why I shouldn't swing: I could fall to my death, make a fool of myself, get rope burn, chafe my behind, swallow a large jungle bug. I'll admit I was reaching. When I finally faced the fear, I could see that the obstacles I was creating weren't that big. Later that night I shared my thinking process with my son. He was blasé and unimpressed as any ten-year-old might be, reminding me that he had done the swing with one hand while hanging upside down. "What's the big deal, mom?" Without missing a beat, he added, "I wonder what I'm going to do for *my* mid-life crisis? Maybe I'll run with the bulls in Pamplona."

I hadn't really thought of our travels or that rope swing as a manifestation of my mid-life crisis. In retrospect, mid-life is the time when we allow, in fact expect ourselves — and are allowed by society — to make massive shifts in our lives. This is when we're supposed to challenge our fears, reassess our choices and do what we've secretly been wanting to do for a long time. These transitions, if done carelessly, can be destructive: think of the stereotypical man or woman leaving a spouse and family, buying the red Ferrari and hitting the road to "freedom." The fallout can be ruined marriages and often a spouse left financially bereft while still holding all the responsibilities of family.

What if we thought about these transitions in a more thoughtful way? What if we started out thinking about freedom *with* family and not freedom *from*? Freedom *with* work and not only the escape from it? What would *that* best-case mid-life scenario look like? How can we reset our lives, address any lingering resentments from a life not fully lived, and embrace a jump into the unknown?

The story of the rope swing is the story of all of our fears. It encompasses the tales we tell ourselves about everything that could possibly go wrong. It's about the "whys" and the "shouldn'ts" that fill our mental baggage when we're faced with a new path, and it shows us how easily we can talk ourselves out of welcoming change. That swing didn't take away my fear of heights, but it reminded me that I was on the right the path of growth, and sharing precious time with my son.

As you leave this chapter, I suggest you try an exercise. Think of the rope swing and the amazing valley below with the Amazon River snaking through the landscape. Then make this story yours. Your story might not include a fear of heights; maybe it's a fear of getting sick while traveling, or getting lost, or not knowing what comes next. Maybe your fear is not being in control.

I invite you to walk through the possibilities, even considering worst-case scenarios — maybe you end up hating travel, and you want to go home. The beautiful thing to keep in mind is that you can always go back, no matter how far you've gone or how long you've been away. Your decision does not need to be permanent. However, most travelers will tell you that even if the journey is short, you won't return the same person.

Aiden swings out over the Amazon River in Peru.

Jacqui and Daniel New

Overcoming Fear to Take the First Step

"If we could just go back and tell ourselves 'It's all fine and easy,' and just take that step and go, we would."

Australians Jacqui and Daniel had been working towards buying a house and accumulating more material things — new cars and more electronics — when they realized they were on the wrong path. "It wasn't really what we wanted to do. We've always wanted to travel," said Jacqui.

They'd been inspired by travels they did together as a young couple, including a honeymoon to Cuba, and wanted their children, Ollie, 13, and Milla, 10, to experience the world.

When the couple came to a crossroads in their careers, they took the funds they'd saved for a deposit on a home and decided to travel instead.

"Dan was in the shower one day and says, 'Hey, why don't we pack our bags, sell everything we own and take off?' So that's what we did," she said.

For the next two years the family traveled with only their carry-on backpacks. They began their journey in Asia, where they spent about nine months before traveling through Europe the following year. Then they made it to the United States, driving through 29 states before flying to Mexico, learning important lessons along the way.

One of their biggest lessons? To slow down. "We moved way too fast. We're from Australia so we had all this pent up travel angst. In over two years we've been to more than 40 countries! If we were to do it again, we would buy an around-the-world ticket, go and have a taste of everything, and then slow down and actually just live a little."

Jacqui and Dan had some initial difficulty landing on a good education program, which is common among families when they first leave traditional schooling. Many parents will tell you, there is no one-size-fits-all where education is concerned, and each family tends to have its own process of unlearning. That said, and despite their extensive planning and spreadsheets, Jacqui said she wished she had researched even more schooling options, given the amount of information now available.

They ultimately landed on a mixture of classical and project-based learning, with a strong emphasis on math. Other lessons came about organically, with the diversity of cultures and countries making an impact. Ollie fell in love with the colors of India; Milla loved France.

Jacqui's insights on food access in America were illuminating.

"The cost of food in the US is so high, not only in the supermarkets but in cafes and restaurants, we can't afford it. We can't afford to go to lunch and spend $60USD on a meal. Most of the time we had breakfast at the hotel, which was crappy waffles with crappy sauce. Then we'd have takeaway for lunch and for dinner. At Hardees you get a meal for six bucks. We'd get one meal that could feed two people and we'd share it, because they are huge meals. By the end of our stay we felt really sick, and full of sugar. It was really difficult for the three months we were in the US."

After the US they flew to Mexico, where affordable, fresh produce is abundant. They chose the location to connect with other families at a Worldschooling conference, and before that they spent time in an ad hoc community of families called Stone Soup, where like-minded travelers came together to share experiences and advice. The exchanges were essential, Jacqui said. It became apparent just how different each person's journey was.

"Before we left our biggest challenge was fear. If we could just go back and tell ourselves 'It's all fine and easy', and just take that step and go, we would. We planned and planned, including spreadsheets, on where we were going to go and how long we were going to spend. And it all changed. Once we left, as soon as we took that step, we weren't stressed."

They had spent so much time worrying about whether they were doing the right thing only to find that their children loved the experiences.

"It's been one of the best experiences ever. The kids love it. They don't ever want to go back to traditional schooling."

Their advice to other traveling families is that no two travel journeys will look alike. Everybody's way of traveling is uniquely their own, so whether you take short trips with your family while keeping a home base or move abroad for years, the clear message is to travel more and worry less.

"Long-term travel is great for us and works for us. Any way that you can bring travel, including the experience of travel and different cultures into your life, is amazing. So give it a go."

Essential Travel Items

I wouldn't leave without my laptop and my phone.

Ollie wouldn't leave without his Kobo e-reader, because he reads voraciously. Dan would say his shoes. He's been wearing the same pair for two and a half years, so we've just replaced them.

Milla likes a little bit of variety in her clothing, but she probably liked to bring along her big teddy bear. It's not that big, but it's a comforting, soft toy.

Mascara. I found when I first went away, I left with very few beauty products and I struggled a little bit because I couldn't make myself up. I know that sounds kind of shallow, but I felt like I wasn't myself because I couldn't put on a little bit of mascara. Although I can live without it, it does make me feel better while traveling on the road.

Chapter 3

Attitude is Everything

"Travel is fatal to prejudice, bigotry, and narrow-mindedness, and many of our people need it sorely on these accounts. Broad, wholesome, charitable views of men and things cannot be acquired by vegetating in one little corner of the earth all one's lifetime." – Mark Twain

Years ago, when I began to talk of our impending adventures, people were excited for me. They also started projecting their fears onto us. Wasn't I afraid? Where would I go? Where would Aiden go to school? Didn't I fear for his safety/social life/growth in general? How would I afford to do it? What if my house didn't rent? I had traveled enough to know that the majority of these questions weren't really for me; they were projections of other people's worries about travel and change. Sure, folks wanted to understand the logistics, but when I gave practical answers to what I saw as unnecessary fears — or simply said, "I don't know yet" — there was a look of terror on their faces.

The truth is, the unknown scares us. It feels bigger, more daunting, and often impossible. It's also where we have our greatest adventures, and in my personal experience, growth. This is part of what travel inspires: a flexibility and awareness that we don't always have to have the answers. In fact, sometimes the greatest gift is simply embracing a new question.

When I say attitude is everything, this isn't some fortune cookie platitude. Attitude is the armor that will keep you whole as you begin your journey. I say this because during challenging times, it may be hard to remember why you've made the decision to travel. As you start out, there will be numerous times you may doubt your own decisions, and fear for your children's happiness and well-being. Even if you start out with confidence, you will encounter naysayers, including close family members and friends whose opinions you respect and appreciate, who will tell you any or all of the following: you are escaping reality, being irresponsible with money, destabilizing your child and disrupting his or her education, destroying your work potential, pricing yourself out of a real estate market, and more. Believe me, I've heard it all. This is the moment to remember why you are choosing your own path.

Traveling is about attitude, and it's also about intuition. When we lack our more familiar indicators, our intuition might be our best guide to tell us what's right. It's a fantastic opportunity to build trust in ourselves and our gut feelings, and also to trust other people. This is The Jump — that proverbial leap of faith, where we have to trust the stranger who is offering help, or know that an unfamiliar food won't kill us. It's what makes this journey so rich.

It doesn't mean that things won't go wrong. They most likely will. Your kids will complain endlessly; you might get sick on the road; you might be robbed or even hurt. Of course, these things might happen while you are in your own town or city too. You will need preparation, common sense and street smarts, so that potential obstacles become mere bumps in a long road of experiences.

Here's the good part: what travel teaches again and again is that most people everywhere are good and kind, generous and helpful. And people are far kinder to children in most places outside the United States, in my experience. They support families and embrace mothers, in both policies and personal actions. Children are cherished and also given freedom. In Mexico children are often out late with their families; in Indonesia, they run and play near busy streets, always under the watchful eye of adults. In France, a family with children can step to the head of the line – and if you're flying out of Charles de Gualle Airport, this can be the difference between a made or missed flight.

I'll never forget working in Cambodia, in a home that held a Montessori school on its bottom floor – and an open pool in the yard. Since Aiden also was attending this school, I asked the owner if she could put a barrier around the pool to keep any young children from falling in. The owner looked confused, so I tried to explain.

"There are so many drownings in America when children walk or fall into pools such as these. Aren't you afraid one of these school children might drown?" I asked her. She looked me right in the eye and with full seriousness answered, "Cambodian children not so stupid." I still laugh at this response. She did end up posting an old woman in a chair by the pool, who I assumed also could not swim. But the woman was clearly there just for me; each of these children had already been taught the danger of water.

So rather than spending energy fearing for your child, take comfort that travel more commonly broadens their mind. It builds resilience and flexibility, and serves as a counter to bigotry and small mindedness. Your child may not remember the specifics of that historical monument or museum collection, but somewhere in their cellular structure, they will remember the variety of faces they have seen, the kids they played with who spoke a different language, the various foods they ate. They will remember the people who lived in houses so different from their own, and how they spent their days. They will realize there are a million ways to live in the world, people who look different from them in any numbers of ways and shades, and that any one of them or all of them can and do become friends.

A group of Worldschooling friends on a boat in Indonesia.

Alicia E.

Embracing Simplicity for a Calmer Life

"We've learned that living with less stuff makes life nicer, calmer, cleaner and less stressful."

Alicia's world was turned upside down at age 34 when her husband died suddenly. The mother of three from Minnesota said the loss made her reevaluate her life and confirmed that spending time with family was her priority. But she couldn't imagine how a single mom with three children working full time could swing more time with her children. That's when her own mother suggested she move abroad. She quit her job working 12-hour nursing shifts, packed twelve suitcases, and moved to Cuenca, Ecuador.

Her kids took online classes and learned to be more organized. They lived on social security, investments and savings. Fewer material belongings made for a calmer space, she said.

"We've learned that living with less stuff makes life nicer, calmer, cleaner and less stressful. My kids also entertain themselves. They caught crabs on the beach yesterday and today have been painting seashells — no electronic entertainment here!"

Ultimately she was successful in reaching her goal of spending time together as a family. Plus, they live a healthier lifestyle, traveling and being creative. The children's bond with their mother is stronger, they're more multicultural, speak another language and are familiar with different customs, and know how to get around more independently than their cousins back in the US, Alicia said.

Her advice to others? "Just go! Do it! All the things you think you need to plan in advance or that you have planned out (like schools) end up changing the moment you land. Just roll with it." Also, don't rent a place until you arrive at your location, she advises.

"For example, this month we are visiting the coast of Peru and Ecuador and the rental we are currently in has light switches at my eye level (impossible for kids). Other rentals have countertops made for the 4'9" Ecuadorian ladies and my back kills after washing dishes."

Essential Travel Items

A power strip for long trips. Many international airports do not have charging areas and by having a power strip, not only do you get to charge your items, but you make tons of friends by sharing with others.

Chapter 4

Assessing Your Life,
a Journaling Exercise

The decision to travel with your family should begin with some basic questions. Really basic.

I'd like you to do an exercise:

Before we talk destination or budget, take some time and think about your life. Start to write — without judgment or edits — about what you'd like more of, and where things might not be working as well.

Are you happy with your life? If no, or even yes, how would you like it to be different?

Are you happy with the schooling of your children? Have you considered other educational possibilities? How much are you willing to stretch in this area?

Are you spending enough time with your loved ones? What does that time look like?

Do you have enough time for yourself?

Do you want to travel more? Do you want to learn new languages?

How is your current health? What is your level of stress?

Do you have the quality of life that you want, with enough money to afford to eat well, sign your kids up for afterschool classes, or hire a babysitter if you want a night on the town?

Imagine yourself on your deathbed reviewing your life, your parenting, your job and relationships, and imagine what, if any, regrets you might have. Write them down.

Think practically about your work life and your finances.

Are you happy with your work? Is it work that can be done remotely? If not, what kinds of skills do you have that might be transportable?

Do you prioritize finances and saving with an eye on retiring at 65 or later?

How much money do you need to live on? Can you imagine living on less? Are you good at saving?

Think deeply and honestly, and allow yourself to venture into the fantasyland of "what if". *What would a perfect life look like? What could it look like?* Write it all down.

When we were offered a chance to go
dog sledding in Switzerland, we jumped at it.

Rebecca Eichler and Paul Carlino

Reinventing Yourself on the Road

Paul and Rebecca spent 20 years of their former lives in Alexandria, Virginia, where Paul was a tax attorney with the Internal Revenue Service in Washington, DC, and Rebecca had her own law practice. In 2015 the couple took their two kids out of school for a year, to drive an old van through Central America.

Ask Rebecca how this adventure came to be and she recalls an Australian she met when she was 20 years old studying in France. He had around-the-world tickets and was traveling for a year. "It totally blew my mind that people could do that. I wanted to do it too."

The next decades of her life simply happened in a traditional way: grad school, a job and a house, a marriage and kids. Traveling for a year just didn't fit anywhere. Rebecca and Paul managed a trip to Ecuador in the summer of 2008. There, on a sandy beach, they met a woman who was traveling with her two teenagers for a year. The same impulse she had after meeting the Australian was magnified. "You can do that? You have two teenagers and you're allowed to pull them out of school and travel for a year? It was mind blowing," Rebecca said. "That's when I told Paul I wanted to do that too."

They saved for several years and when the time came to leave, Paul asked for — and received — a year's leave of absence from the IRS, with a promise that he would return. For Rebecca, the leave was a compromise; what she really wanted was to permanently move overseas. However, a year would be a good start. Their children Maya and Jonah were 12 and 10 when they set out.

"We did go back, but then the wheels started to kind of fall off of that life," Paul said about the end of their tour. But we're getting ahead of ourselves.

They bought an old VW Westfalia van and named it Wesley, after a character in the film, *The Princess Bride*. They poured in many thousands more dollars to design it for a traveling family of four, adding a refrigerator and solar panels, though resisting the addition of an air conditioner unit. This would play into their budget in hotel rooms down the road.

They planned a budget of $100 a day, or $3000 a month for a family of four. Mexico was the most affordable country; each country got increasingly expensive as they moved south, with Costa Rica and Panama being the most costly of their trip. They kept well to the budget with 142 nights of their 340-day trip spent in hostels or hotels. They spent fewer nights than they expected in the van because it was too hot and humid. Paul spent over $1000 on beer. #priorities

Online school was a struggle while traveling, Rebecca admitted, but their daughter managed to read 100 books on the road, and their son had already been taking advanced classes, so he never fell behind.

Many months later the family landed in Panama, where people traveling overland (usually in a car or camper van) have to decide whether to ship their vehicles across the Panama Canal and continue onward to South America, or turn back. With limited time remaining and promises made to return home, they turned back.

"The day that we turned around in Panama, I cried all day," Rebecca recalled. Even though they had three months of travel left, it felt like the end of the road, she said. It meant going back.

Once they returned home, Rebecca fell into a deep depression. It wasn't just that the people they met on the road showed them a life abroad was entirely possible; she also mourned the time they spent together as a family. Now Paul was back at work and the kids had school, but Rebecca was more autonomous with her time. After spending quite literally every moment of the past year with her family, she was alone at home in a life she didn't care for anymore. "It was awful. I was depressed for a very long time."

"For me, I was trying to fit back into a life as a different person. I thought I could slide back into the life that I was living before, but I had changed. I didn't have the same view of things. It just didn't fit me anymore."

The depression got so extreme that Rebecca was having difficulty getting out of bed. Then came a phone call from a mother they had met on the road. Would she and the kids like to join them in Colombia? Rebecca jumped and took Maya and Jonah down to Colombia for a month while Paul worked. Once she returned, her mind was set. "We've got to move overseas."

This time, however, they would be going without jobs. Luckily, their penchant for savings and general financial savvy paved the way. The smartest thing they had done, Paul said, was to pay off their mortgage.

"We bought this house in a sketchy area, early in our careers. We still had student loans from grad school." At that time, Rebecca was making $30,000 as an immigration attorney for Catholic Charities, and Paul was a new government employee. Both were at the very early end of their career earnings, yet they maintained the same standard of living even as they progressed in their careers and their earnings grew. As they made more, they simply saved more, resisting what is commonly called "lifestyle creep," which means the act of expanding your spending to meet any increased income.

"We didn't move, we didn't buy a bigger place, which was a really smart thing that we did. We had only paid $170,000 for our house."

They quit their jobs and decided to move to a town in Mexico where they had made friends during their travels. Rental income from their US house eventually became their primary income source, especially given that the "sketchy area" had now morphed into a trendy and desirable part of DC. In fact, it paid not only their rent once they arrived back in Mexico, but tuition for two teens in private school.

Paul began taking on writing projects and helping people with taxes. Rebecca launched a retreat workshop in Mexico teaching Spanish to lawyers and activists, specifically around immigration issues.

Friends still ask them about the dangers in Mexico and feel concerned for their safety. Violence certainly was on their mind, particularly while driving, but a foreigner with foreign plates has a kind of pass that local people may not, Rebecca learned. Having worked on immigration issues for years, she was well aware of the privilege of a US passport, and relative ease of crossing borders.

When people asked if she had been worried driving from Virginia to Panama, she quipped, "Yeah, I'm really worried about having to drive through Texas with all the guns." Added Paul, "Before we left Virginia, there was a mass shooting at a church in South Carolina, but nobody told us not to drive through South Carolina."

Once they crossed the border and for the year that followed, they never felt physically threatened. Instead, they fell in love with Mexico and its culture. Sure, there was a shake down or two with cops asking for bribes (which they refused to pay), and a few clothing items stolen — their son's t-shirt and a bathing suit from a laundry line while they slept, a pair of flip flops from outside the van door. Paul smiles at the memory.

"If those are the two worst things that are going to happen, I'll do it again any day."

Essential Travel Items

A Van! For a woman who says she initially abhorred the idea of being trapped in a car with her husband and two kids, I came to love it. "It's my favorite place to be."

Supplies for the road include a cast iron skillet and good sharp knives. "I like to cook and a sharp knife is important to me. Now I can't imagine flying and not being able to take my knives with me!"

Definitely electronics. Everybody having a screen is key.

A power strip: We ended up buying a power strip because some of the places we stayed at never had enough outlets for all four of us to charge our phones and computers at the same time.

For internet connection we bought SIM cards in every country. They were cheap, easily available and very easy to load.

Crucial overlanding apps included <u>maps.me</u> (so you can download city maps and use them offline), and iOverlander, an essential app for any roadtripping families or individuals.

Other helpful sites include <u>boondockerswelcome.com</u> at $80/year (at this writing), which lists safe, free sites to camp with hosts across the US. <u>Outdoorsy.com</u> connects local RV, motorhome, and campervan owners with families wanting to rent them.

Chapter 5

The Time is Now

"It's not the years in your life that count. It's the life in your years."

I've always prioritized experiences over material belongings, it's simply how I lived my life. From a young age I remember a brown scrap of paper, small and carefully taped to the wall of my mother's home with a quotation attributed to Adlai Stevenson, though I imagine the phrase was spoken by others long before him: "It's not the years in your life that count. It's the life in your years." I read the quote every morning as I made my way to the breakfast table and every evening as I made my way back to bed. It made an impression.

This doesn't mean that I don't value financial responsibility or stability. I maintain a stable home in the town where I grew up, and I have included a chapter on finances in this book. For me, the quote is about having the frame of mind to see if your material priorities (e.g. a college fund) are blinding you to your real priorities (the reason for such a fund: your children and their futures).

When you think about long term travel, there are a million reasons why the time isn't right, and some of those reasons can feel very valid. The narrative most people embrace goes something like this: I'll work my entire life to sock away funds so one day I'll be able to enjoy those funds, and share some adventures with the people I love.

To be clear, that day just might not come.

This isn't some doomsday prediction, but a reality of life. Who hasn't heard about the person who, just months after retiring, has a heart attack and dies? Who hasn't heard of a young life tragically cut short before any of his or her dreams could take flight? Or the person who saved his entire life for retirement, only to find himself struck by illness that prohibited the travels or creations of his dreams?

More often than not, the people I met on the road had their "aha" moment after a severe jolt in their lives. It took a life tragedy to shake them out of an everyday slog — be it illness, a near death experience, or the death of a loved one. It sounds like some bumper sticker slogan: live life to the fullest because you never know what tomorrow may bring. But for many people interviewed in this book, such truisms became their truth. They lost loved ones, got sick or divorced, were fired from jobs they thought they'd have forever. The security they had taken for granted suddenly disappeared.

The reality is that it isn't one thing or another. It's not 'work yourself to death so you can retire at 65 and finally take a vacation' versus 'sell everything and go traveling until every penny is spent.' There is a middle path that focuses on your desire and lays the groundwork to do it responsibly. Travel *and* financial awareness. Adventure *and* responsibility. Life enriching experiences with family *and* securing a future for your children. Fate meets planning. Luck meets an open mind and opportunity.

When I was working as a foreign journalist in Iraq many years ago it bothered me a great deal when, every time I told someone of a plan or tried to schedule a meeting, their response was, *"Inshallah,"* meaning, "God Willing." I felt it might be a curse, to cast some doubt on my ability to reach my goal. I soon realized that culturally it was simply the way they saw the world: we exist, eat, breathe, work and love only by the grace of God — and at any moment our fates can change.

The time, therefore, is right now.

So much to learn in the Galápagos Islands, Ecuador.
Charles Darwin visited the volcanic archipelago in
1835 and from observing the islands' species later
developed his theory of evolution. Here Aiden is
joined by a fellow swimmer – an iguana.

Cindy B.

Give Yourself Permission

"We had to press pause on what we were doing so we could have this new opportunity, this new adventure."

Cindy defines herself as a radical unschooler. She and her five-year-old son Noel were living in New York City where she ran a successful business and rented out an apartment for additional income. Travel had always been part of the larger plan; when her husband died, she realized it was time to put that plan into motion.

At first she dreamed of crossing the United States in an Airstream. Then she became overwhelmed by the logistics of it — not to mention how she felt being a black woman traveling across North America.

"Once I started to map out where we would go, the entire South was out of the picture for me. I just knew that being a single black female in the South was not a possibility. It is a scary place. So I couldn't go any-where south of Virginia — or not even Virginia. So, what, the Northeast? Then we'd have to go across the country to the West. It started to not make sense. That's also part of the reason the Airstream idea was off the table."

Cindy embraced the idea that she would travel the United States another time; for now, she wanted dif-ferent cultures. While her son was young, she wanted him to get outside of being and identifying with being an American.

The family had been on short trips before — one- or two-week vacations here and there — but long term-travel was a different animal. When she saw a notice for a Worldschooling conference, it became the springboard for their trip to Mexico. She was able to rent out two properties she owned in New York, which easily financed her travels.

Cindy said she always wanted her son to have an epic and unusual childhood, but she wasn't sure what that meant. She knew homeschooling would be part of the plan. The rest, she couldn't yet see.

Of course, "epic" to an adult is very different than to a child. So one of her challenges was conveying the exceptional aspect of their experience to a five-year-old who didn't really understand why they were on the road at all.

"I basically explained to him that because we aren't going to a traditional school this is how we're going to learn. We're going to learn from the world and the world will be our classroom," she told him. They couldn't just sit in their apartment in New York City; they had to get out.

Slowly, the reality began seeping in. The larger issue for her son was access to more technology. Already at five, Noel was a serious gamer, so it was up to mom to research and figure out numerous ways he could game while they were away. "The next time we go out on a big trip I'll make sure we have a really good WiFi connection and we'd bring the Xbox. Noel wants the full experience and that's really important for his happiness."

The other important aspect for them was being able to cook. After two weeks in Mexico they still were cooking and eating the same foods they ate at home. It helped her son feel some continuity.

Cindy says information is key. "When I feel passionate about something, I read every book, every magazine, I Google everything. So I know what it is, I get a feel for it. I read reviews," she said. "Once you're armed with information, you feel powerful." Her advice to others would be to do the same: get lots of information, go with your instincts, and allow the momentum to help you progress to the next step.

"I'm doing it, we're doing it here, so don't let that hold you back. If you are one adult and one child or one adult and many children, it is possible to do, and you can figure it out. You don't have to have two adults in order to make something like this a possibility," she said.

Luckily, she had no naysayers telling her that travel was too dangerous or advising her not to go. On the contrary, people told her they were jealous. She suspects they understood the American cultural context she was trying to avoid.

It's the baggage that comes with being an African American that Cindy was starting to feel — and of burdening her son with it.

"I wanted to remove him from the baggage. I want him to be a global citizen, and to know where he came from, but not to carry that baggage with him as he lives. We don't feel it in Mexico. I'm sure Mexico has its issues, but it's not that baggage."

She also appreciates that her son is surrounded by people who look like him. "Here, everyone is brown, and that's huge."

Essential Travel Items

Electronics, including an Xbox and the ability to boost WiFi.

Chapter 6

Set Your Priorities

I once dated a wonderful man who was recently divorced and had two children. He made literally ten times the amount I earned in a year. Just his Christmas bonus was more than my annual salary. Our children loved each other and we always had fun together. One day, I devised a plan that I thought could be a wonderful adventure. We could take all three kids to Legoland in San Diego for a long weekend. I'd found a hotel and an amazing flight deal. When I excitedly laid out the plans, my sweetie scoffed, "That would cost close to $1000!" I was speechless. The cost would have been equal for both of us, yet I was willing to spend this amount for a chance to have time together, away from home and in a place where the kids would create memories of a lifetime. To me, it was worth the price.

When we finally sat down to talk about the cost, he said he couldn't spend money on anything "frivolous" until his children's college funds were paid in full. His kids were six and seven at the time. This experience showed me that many of our decisions are based not at all on whether we can afford them, but where they fall on our list of priorities.

Don't get me wrong: college is important. Retirement and savings is important. An emergency fund is essential. But once you identify a general priority, consider whether there is flexibility and room for growth. Can we fund college *and* have adventures? This friend showed me how easily a "priority" illuminates an excuse and vice versa. His priority erased the possibility for some wonderful, spontaneous experiences. Sadly, it became clear that our priorities were too divergent, and the relationship ended soon thereafter.

I don't write this with judgement. In fact, it was a very eye-opening experience for me to see that this lifestyle is not for everyone. Before this, I simply couldn't imagine that people wouldn't want similar adventures; I figured they just didn't know how to create them. I came to realize that for many people – dare I say most – a week or two at a clean resort or luxury hotel might be enough adventure for one year.

American citizens in particular have not been educated or allowed to think more about flexible work, the importance of time off, or the value of travel generally; for these people, time away translates as a threat to their financial or employment security. Or travel simply isn't important. This book is not for those people. This book for those who have begun to question how best to spend time with family and what a redesigned life might look like. This book is for those who want to live differently.

In Paris, visiting the love lock bridge,
the Pont des Arts, before the locks were removed
due to the structural damage they caused.

Allison Sherman

The Schengen Zone and other Visa Restrictions

"You can't stay indefinitely in most countries. There are visa regulations and it's frustrating."

Allison is funny as heck, and meeting her was the highlight of my first Worldschooling conference. With her slight southern twang, I imagined motivational speaker Brené Brown offering travel tips. Allison and her husband and two daughters left Arizona for Panama in 2014. The plan was to immerse the girls in Spanish language. Allison had previously worked with student exchange programs and figured two years would be the right amount of time to absorb a new language. That was seven years ago.

Her entrepreneurial husband already worked online, running a range of different businesses, including collectibles, a number of domain names and email addresses, and he was part owner of a pharmacy in India. "Basically, he sees a need — mostly a need that he has — and then he fills it," Allison said. With that skill set and income, the family could go anywhere.

One challenge was taking the full-time job of motherhood on the road, then adding to her duties that of travel agent — and therapist — for everyone.

"I feel responsible for all of their happiness. Where do they sleep? Are they getting enough sleep? What do they eat? What are their activities? It feels like a lot of coordination and cruise directing," she said.

Another challenge was that homeschooling didn't feel natural to her or to her daughters, but moving around as much as they did, it was the best option they could find. Allison occasionally enrolled her girls in local schools, more for socialization and cultural knowledge than for academics. With the blessing of local administrators, they would stay for several months, make friends, help fellow students with English, then move on. The girls adored being in school settings for short periods, before happily returning to unstructured learning.

They did become fluent in Spanish and as they left Panama to see many other countries, they increasingly saw how easily people could do more with less. In Dubai, they got used to hearing the call to prayer, and from their time in drought-stricken South Africa, the girls learned to ask questions about resources: Does the next country we're going to have a lot of power outages? Do we need battery-operated fans and lanterns? Is it okay to drink the water here? "They ask questions that they never knew to ask. I couldn't have taught that, and I didn't necessarily teach it either. It was just there."

Colombia topped their list of kid-friendly countries for its family-oriented culture and multitude of parks. Older people sat on benches while kids ran and played. Spain, too, had plazas everywhere, and long promenades, whether by a river, a canyon or a beach.

"We bought the kids scooters in Spain because that's what everybody did. The parents sit and chat at a cafe and the kids ride scooters."

She ranked Amsterdam as the least family-friendly location, because of the Red Light districts and storefront shows. "We don't need to grow up quite that fast by looking at this store. That's not really the homeschool lesson I was looking for today," Allison joked. The Netherlands was the only place that was more expensive for the family than living in the US.

Many families fear a medical mishap on the road, but after many years and their share of medical check-ins – dog bites, mammograms and even a colonoscopy in Panama – Allison said most all her experiences were fine. Doctors often spoke English extremely well and they too wanted their patients to get better. Importantly, there are mothers all over the world who you can ask, mother-to-mother, for help.

"You can get in a taxi and say, 'help me, my finger is bleeding. Can you please take me to the hospital?' And they will. We're human beings. I always felt like I knew where I could go to get help," Allison said. "We have seen medical professionals all over the world with no issues. My daughter has received orthodontic care in five countries, and her smile is beautiful."

One of their most successful travel strategies was making sure each family member had a "turn" to decide where to visit. That way, each child participated and had buy-in to the adventure. One daughter chose Thailand, then both girls wanted to continue their language learning so they returned to a Spanish-speaking country. Eventually it was the youngest child's turn and she wanted to return home to attend a traditional high school. This wish was also honored, and after seven years of travel the family returned to the United States.

"I'm sure we'll keep traveling, but maybe not in the same way. No more lack of home base, nomadic, where-the-wind-blows kind of way. I have a feeling we'll have a home base and maybe take a few more short trips."

Allison's advice to other travelers is not to assume you have to know everything before leaving. The important part is simply taking the first step. "We believe in soft landings, and Panama was our soft landing," she said. Panama uses US currency, it has the same electrical voltage, and there are lots of expats. The time zone was similar to the US, and with basic Spanish knowledge they could read the street signs.

"That was all we had planned. After going to Panama, we felt more confident and we had built up our skills enough to navigate another country." If you don't know where to start but you've been dreaming of one country, Allison suggests starting there. "That's a good dream. Spend some time, meet some people, then think about where you want to go next. One step at a time is really all that's necessary."

She had some other lessons to share as well. "One is, we left more roots back home than we needed. We left a car and we left three very large climate-controlled storage units filled with furniture. After a year we went back and emptied that out. Now we have one very small storage unit with memories and baby books. It might feel emotionally hard to give that away before you know what you're doing, but almost everybody I've talked to would suggest leaving as few roots at home as possible because it gives you more freedom when you're abroad."

Another, and this comes up a lot: you can't stay indefinitely in most countries. "There are visa regulations and it is frustrating. We looked eight ways from Friday on how to stay in Spain and it wasn't possible. We couldn't stay longer than 90 days. We tried, we wanted to stay a year, we wanted to go to school there. I'm sure there are ways, but none of the ways made sense financially to us. We couldn't do it." Part of deciding where to go is to plan for specific events or times of year. "We wanted to be in the Netherlands for the tulips, and we could only stay in Europe for thirty more days. We had to time it just right. Some people think, 'we'll just go and we'll see what it's like.' You really have to look at your visa regulations."

Other things to consider include weather, how to get a driver's license (if you don't already have an international driver's license), and of course, how you plan to access money.

"The part that feels the hardest and the most uncomfortable is right before you leave to travel. It actually gets a lot better once you go because then you have a new set of challenges that you're focused on, such as getting your phone to work or looking for apartments. At that point you feel like you're moving forward, but before you go, it's hard to move forward because you just haven't left yet."

Essential Travel Items

My own blanket and pillow. They're familiar and they help me sleep, which is so critical when so much around you is new. You need that replenishing time when you sleep.

The other important time of my day is in the morning. I get up a little earlier than the family and I have coffee and tend to check in with my family online. I carry a very small French press, coffee pot.

Those things bookmark my day so that whatever happens in between the morning coffee and the nighttime getting under my blanket, can be tolerated a little bit more. At least I know how my morning is going to begin and I know how my day is going to end.

Chapter 7

Build Your Community

You've read these chapters and you feel the calling. You've always wanted to travel, even if it feels like such adventures are for other people. Still, you want to move forward. You've dreamed of taking your children out of school for a year of exploration and eye- and heart-opening experiences. Now hearing stories of other families' successes suddenly makes the dream feel within reach. If this is you, go ahead and congratulate yourself; you've accomplished by far the most difficult step of all!

You're starting to give yourself permission.

That first step of simply allowing yourself to consider this adventure, means you are starting to take control of your life and look those doubters and naysayers in the eyes. You know the ones. I mentioned them in previous chapters: those who smear their anxiety onto you, worry about your job, your house, your future, the health of your children and maybe have reservations about your own mental health as well. They're the ones who project their own fears onto you because in many

67

cases they have the same unmet desires, and they really and truly begrudge your bravery. As Brené Brown might say, you are the one about to enter the arena, and no one outside that space should be allowed to project their criticism and fears onto you. Stay strong and focused and congratulate yourself for moving forward. The practical aspects of travel are challenging, but these steps pale in comparison to that big first step.

The next critical step is to surround yourself, even if only virtually, with like-minded people — those also in the arena. These individuals and families have taken the leap or are in the planning stages, or simply have a similar dream. Whether you plan to leave for a month, a year, or a lifetime, these families are there to share information and support your efforts, and can allay fears if and when they arise.

In order to nourish and grow your dream, I would right away recommend reading the blogs, listening to podcasts, or watching TikTok, Instagram and YouTube videos of any number of families who are doing or have done what you are hoping to do. There are hundreds of families leading the way and many have amazing tales to tell, some of which appear in this book. Take in the stories of these travelers. Regardless of the location or mode of travel you choose, you will find a story that resonates for you. Just remember: You're not alone, so get connected. There is not likely a question you will ask that hasn't been asked before — and garnered dozens of responses. Travelers want to help you.

I can't list them all but I'll note some of my favorite resources, many of which inspired me and fed my own travel dreams. I'll begin by suggesting my own website, where I've written about my travels with my son: adventuringatoz.com

There is a growing number of groups forming around the term Worldschooling. A search for these groups on Facebook will bring up dozens, including:
Worldschooling.com
WorldschoolingCentral.com and worldschoolingdirectory.com, both by Karen King (interviewed in these pages)
ProjectWorldschool.com by Lainie Liberti (interviewed in these pages)
Worldschoolersconnect
WeAreWorldschoolers.org
Worldtravelfamily.com
Worldschoolerexchange.com
Worldschoolinghub.com
Worldschoolpopuphub.com

Thewanderingdaughter.com – by Astrid Vinji and Clint Bush (interviewed in these pages)

Enlightenedglobetrekker.com – Happy and Enlightening Traveling Adventures

Dreamtimetraveler.com –Teenage Life-schooler Traveling the World by Réka Kaponay. Kaponay also is author of the fantasy fiction novel, Dawn of the Guardian.

Travelbabbo.com – Eric has been posting for years about travel on Facebook, Instagram, and on his blog.

EntreFamily.com – Life, travel and work for family-minded entrepreneurs.

Jenn Miller writes a weekly blog about homeschool education @jenn.lately (also interviewed in these pages).

PanAmerican Travelers Association on Facebook – Essential travel information for families traveling overland, usually in their own vehicles (aka Overlanders).

Karen and Cameron King

Mixing Full Time Travel and Work

"Don't let people get in your head."

Karen and her husband Cameron left Australia with their two kids, 8 and 14, for what they thought would be a short-term adventure. She was a cake decorator when she read Tim Ferriss's book, *The 4-Hour Work Week* — a kind of bible among Worldschoolers — and realized maybe there were other ways to make a living, and other ways to live a life.

"I'd been working so hard for five years. I was really concerned that the stress I was under was going to make me sick," she said. "I just thought, life's too short." In the beginning of Tim Ferriss's book he asks the question, "If money were no object, what would you do?" Karen's answer: I would travel. Beyond that she was so tired, she couldn't think of any other responses. By the end of the book, she learned the term "location in-dependence," which means one's work and life is not dependent on a specific location.

Karen and Cam both knew they wanted to travel with their kids early, instead of waiting until they retired. So when their kids were in 5th grade and kindergarten, and both kids began to struggle in school, they jumped.

Karen's mantra became Don't Hesitate. "I know that's really easy to say. I think so many people talk them-selves out of it because in the beginning it feels so hard. It's so far out of people's comfort zones that it can be difficult to picture. Imagine selling everything off in a culture where you're judged by the quality of your car and the size of your house. I think it's a matter of not letting other people get into your head."

It's a big step to break away from the norm, she ad-mits, but long-term travel is becoming more and more normal for so many families. Based on conversations she's had with other travelers, there are few families that regret their travels, whether they leave for three months or six months, whether they sell everything, or rent their home for a year. "Give it a go. There's really not a lot of downsides," she said.

The King family financed their first two years from savings, having sold everything to leave with a clean slate and full pockets. An early lesson was about materialism. Each family member travels with a seven-kilo (15.43 lbs.) bag of personal belongings — carry-on luggage only — plus a communal bag for electronics. They avoid expensive hotels and high-end luxuries, relying instead on the quality of their experiences.

"Buying a new car brings you happiness for a couple of months, but then you're paying off debt for years. That same money can take you around the world and create memories that stay with you forever. It's so much about priorities, isn't it?"

Education was initially a challenge, with the family ultimately embracing unschooling, meaning their kids' education is completely open, based on what they see in their travels and what they experience. They don't do any formal book work at all. She describes a day: "Today we saw the baby turtles and that brought up questions. Now we might go and watch documentaries or we might go research more. The information sticks so much more because we've been there, we've seen it, and it means more to us."

Watching her kids learn according to their own interests has taken some of the unschooling insecurity away. Still, transitioning to this mode after formal education isn't easy; most parents have been trained in a traditional system, and no parent wants to negatively impact their children's possibilities of later success. But success shows up in different ways. Karen's tween daughter radiates a sense of worldliness and openness; she can speak with people half her age, or four times. Her confidence is boundless.

Then there's money. Luckily, entrepreneurship is nothing new to Karen — her projects have included decorating cakes, managing Airbnbs, organizing conferences, and eventually creating group tours for traveling families. One of her first big ventures was planning a group trip for eleven families — 39 people in total — to the Indonesian islands of Bali and Gili Air.

"It was absolutely amazing. It's all about community, making new friends, learning from each other, watching the kids make friends and interact. We're going to run more trips as a result."

Additional group trips were planned for the pyramids of Egypt and yet another to visit the Great Wall of China.

Through these projects, the biggest challenge was maintaining a work discipline in what often feels like a long vacation. It's about practice, she said, and trying things until you get it right. In fact, Karen's latest venture was helping women launch the technical aspects of their own remote businesses. Each of these projects feed her larger goal to help build this remote, traveling family of colleagues and friends.

The good thing, she insists, is that travel is not nearly as costly as people think. "I always hear people say, 'I wish I could do it, but I couldn't afford it' or 'you must have won the lotto.'" Yet there are people traveling on $1000 a month. Karen's own family of four managed for about $2800 a month. To put this in context, their lives in Australia — an expensive country by most measures — had a budget of roughly $3500 a month for a basic lifestyle (roughly 4500 Australian dollars). By traveling the world full time, they reduced their costs by $700 a month!

Karen's greatest tip for keeping expenses low was to use the housesitting membership site called trusted-housesitters.com. For a small annual fee ($150 at this writing), travelers can find opportunities for free accommodation in exchange for caring for someone's home and pets while the homeowner is away. It entails building an engaging profile and then submitting a well-crafted application that convinces the homeowner you're the best choice to care for their home and beloved pets.

Their housing costs were slashed, while the family also benefited from living in a welcoming environment: "We have a home, a kitchen, and pets. It's a real family type environment. We can stay longer, too, because quite often the stays are four to six weeks."

During their first two years of travel, they went wherever the most interesting house sits were located, including South Korea, Mexico, Spain, and all through Southeast Asia, for a total of more than 40 house sits in three and a half years.

The best sits — the mansion in the UAE or the five-star suite in China — will likely have many applications, so the key, she says, is building up your profile and then making sure you leave the residences better than you found them.

"Clearly, it's given us opportunities and experiences that we wouldn't have otherwise had." Not only that, connecting with animals can be great for kids. "I think we've had 55 dogs in the last three years."

Essential Travel Items

A 10-port USB hub. "It's such a simple thing, but it's a powerful one and very good quality. It comes with us everywhere."

The other item we travel with is a small, voice-activated hub device called Google Home. Wherever we go, we plug it in and use it as an incredible learning tool.

"Instead of going on your phone or your laptop to Google something, we now have Google that's voice activated."

Chapter 8

Where Should We Go?

I find it amusing when people post the question on travel message boards: "Where should I travel with my family?" I understand that for some people even launching that question into the abyss is a huge accomplishment. It is a confirmation of a desire, a kind of fishing lure into the sea of traveling possibilities. Yet there is no way to answer this without more information.

The reality is that once you've decided you want to travel, you yourself will have to narrow things down. There are 195 countries (197 if you include Vatican City and Palestine) on six main continents, and many of these countries are so vast and varied they are like continents in themselves. In other words, the world is a very big place. Obviously, people want to know where other families have gone and what their experiences have been. However, each person or family has different interests, needs for security, and certainly different budgets.

Here are some questions to ask yourself when contemplating your first destination:

What is your budget?

There are certain regions in the world where your dollar will stretch much further than others. Mexico and Central America, for example, are far less expensive than Europe. Southeast Asian countries like Thailand or Cambodia will cost far less than, say, Japan. There are sites liked <u>NomadList.com</u> or <u>Numbeo.com</u> where you can find detailed comparisons of cost of living in various areas of the world. A big shout out also goes to fellow badass mom Tracy Thompson's "<u>Happy Heart Travel</u>" Facebook page in which she describes her monthly travel budget in wonderful detail. One rule of thumb I've heard from several families is to consider $2000 a month for a family of two, $4000 for a family of four. Obviously, this number can be lower or higher, but it's a good starting point for budgeting purposes.

How long do you plan on traveling? Will it be a short exploration or a yearlong adventure?

Many families start out for three months and sometimes end up traveling for years. Some leave for a year and return home within months. At least have a starting goal and a budget to match.

Do you like warm climates or cold ones?

This will also impact how much luggage you bring. Clothes for cold weather will most often take up more space.

Do you know if the place you want to visit has a rainy season, which perhaps is best to avoid?

I planned to hike the Inca Trail in Peru in February not knowing that it closes in that month for maintenance. The rains also happen to be extremely heavy at this time of year.

Do you speak a foreign language or are you more comfortable where English is widely spoken?

Throughout the world English is a common second language. However, even where it is not spoken, you'd be surprised how easy it is to communicate with gestures and perhaps Google translate.

Do you have a passport that might prohibit you from entering some countries? You should also be aware of the order in which you travel, as certain stamps in your passport might be problematic when you enter another country.

For example, travelers to Cuba often ask that a stamp not be put in their passports due to the US embargo; Israeli stamps can be problematic when visiting some neighboring Arab countries.

Do you want to explore more developed countries and towns, or are you comfortable in less developed countries with fewer creature comforts?

Some travelers prefer higher-end accommodations, familiar architecture and amenities; others are happy sleeping on the bow of a boat.

Do you want to be near water?

Whether lakes, rivers or oceans, there are many bodies of water to choose from.

Do you tend toward big cities or small towns?

Many families say small towns are easier to navigate with small children.

Will you be working on the road and need consistent internet?

Remote towns may have limited WiFi, while busy city centers will almost always have good connectivity.

Is your goal simply to find a community where there are other families with young children?

Perhaps it's not the physical location that calls to you as much as the community that is forming in a given location.

What kind of food do you like?

Food can be as unique as the country itself. I've eaten fried bat wings in Cambodia, snails and frogs in France, and Spam in the US. My son searched for – and found – buttered pasta in each of these locations.

Is hospital proximity a requirement?

Some families might have ongoing medical needs or simply feel more comfortable with a hospital nearby.

How do you like to travel?

Will you be driving or flying to each location? Do you like trains or buses? Is it all about #VanLife?

As you can see, there's a wide range of decisions that can help you focus your planning. Of course none of these decisions is set in stone. Once you've thought more about where you'd like to go and what you'd like to see, you can begin to reach out to others who have experiences in the same region. They will see that you've done a bit of homework, and most people I've encountered are extremely generous in sharing their knowledge and contacts.

A word about language: Many people feel intimidated entering a culture where they don't speak the language. This makes perfect sense. However, most travelers will tell you that there are so many ways to communicate while on the road, and the lack of language skills should never stop you from exploring an area. People are most often kind and generous and try to help you even without a shared language. A kind smile can say as much as any language skill.

That said, I would highly recommend trying to learn basic phrases in the languages of the countries you wish to visit. This includes polite phrases of request for food, facilities, help, thanks, and directions. These phrases show that while you are not fluent, you are at least making an effort to respect another culture, a way of life, and people. Even minor efforts can open doors for you to new experiences and conversations.

A few phrases to learn

It's easy to research a few simple phrases for any country you'd like to visit. You'd be surprised at how a bit of effort goes a long way. Here are just a few phrases every traveler should try in the local language:

Hello
Goodbye
Please
Thank You
Can you help me?
What is your name?
My name is...
How much does this cost?
I am a [insert occupation]

Zoe McAdams

Finding Comfort and Safety Abroad

"If you're making it in the US, I think you can make it just about anywhere else in the world."

Zoe says that when African Americans are considering where to travel, the first questions they are likely to ask are: 'Are there Black people there?' and 'How are we going to be treated?' Zoe has been traveling the world with her two kids, Evelyn, 14, and Silas, 13, for years, and reflects often on the questions.

"It's a legitimate question. But I tell people if you're making it in the US, I think you can make it just about anywhere else in the world!"

International travel is still uncommon in many communities, as it was in Zoe's family. "My family didn't have a history of travel. We traveled to Mississippi in the summers to go home, but we didn't do a lot of international travel. It's different if you're of Jamaican or African heritage, because your family may have migrated all over the world."

Zoe said that discussions about living abroad became more common after the murder of George Floyd (an African American man who was murdered by a white police officer in 2020), and the ongoing police violence and treatment of protesters. Yet African Americans still aren't sure if they'll face hostilities in other places. It's one reason why she landed in Playa Del Carmen, Mexico, which has gained a reputation as a welcoming spot. It's an easy flight from New York, Atlanta or LA, and while Spanish language skills are helpful, they're not necessary. "It's booming with African Americans, especially younger ones," she said.

Zoe and her family had begun their journey six years earlier, initially leaving their Seattle home just to get away over the winter holidays. Then, after she and her husband separated, Zoe and the kids began traveling full time, returning every three months for the children to see their dad. A few years after that, they moved to Malaysia to live full time, where she came to the realization that the rest of the world loves kids.

"You'll be surprised how negative the US is once you get out into the world, especially if you have kids under 10. The rest of the world really adores kids."

In Mexico kids are out all night; in Colombia they're running through restaurants; in Southeast Asia they are always part of family outings. Zoe started realizing that it's not as easy to live in the US and that it doesn't always support families. Additionally, in places like Southeast Asia, it's customary to have help. "The help is generally loving and reasonably priced, and kind of becomes part of your family. For smaller kids, Southeast Asia is a great option to start with."

Zoe cautions families to keep in mind the distinction between visiting and living in a place. Just because you love vacationing somewhere, doesn't mean your family will want to stay long term. Consider the options available for children, such as schooling and extracurricular activities. With each new location Zoe enrolls her kids in classes, in part to get them involved with the local culture. She found that places with a strong middle class offered the best opportunities to her family, and her kids could more easily engage in a variety of sports with local children. Malaysia offered lots of educational opportunities and amenities, and it was safe.

Her kids have grown flexible through travel, and their quality of life on the whole – including more and more relaxed time – is generally better. Plus, they simply can afford to do more.

"The amount of things that we're able to do as far as music lessons, motocross, coding, tutors... all of that stuff is possible because we live abroad. Life in Seattle is extremely expensive, so we've been able to do a lot more outside the US than we would have been able to do in the US." These activities include a wide range of sports, including diving, skiing, biking and surfing. "They have plenty of PE," she says.

As for education, when the kids were under ten they focused on math, reading, and reading comprehension, adding more classes as they got older. At thirteen, her daughter started IGSCE testing and had tutors. IGSCE, International General Certificate of Secondary Education, is an internationally recognized testing system that's particularly good for those not in a traditional education system. Her son did similar studies the following year.

Zoe works as a research librarian online, and has been able to fund their lifestyle by traveling slowly and sticking to a $2000 a month budget. She does this by planning her locations — Asia and Latin America are less expensive than Europe, for example — and making sure to rent places longer term.

The cost of renting a place for one to three months can be far less than what is initially advertised, and there's always room for negotiations, especially during low seasons. Establishing a budget on the front end helps her determine where they can go and how long they can stay. She also saves money by not carrying a lot of luggage, not having a car or other amenities Americans might take for granted, like a dryer. All of this holds down her expenses and allows her to travel longer. She calls travel 'the great shake down,' showing you how little you really need in your daily life — and also the ongoing costs of having so many material items. "We don't just pay to acquire things, we pay to maintain them until we pay to replace them."

When asked if Zoe sees herself returning to the US, her answer is unequivocal.

"Never, never, never, never. There's really nothing pulling me back to the US except that my parents are elderly, but I can keep coming to visit."

Her advice to parents starting to look at living abroad is that some places are easier than others, but if a certain place calls to you, you should heed that call. "Loving it will go a long way when you start to think about traveling." She especially wants to encourage other single mothers.

"There are tons of single mothers traveling. If you're a woman who thinks Mexico is scary or Thailand is scary, well yes, the world is a scary place for women. It *is* and it isn't. With regular precautions you can be fine traveling with your kids, and it is a real option for single and young mothers. It's a real option for older mothers. There are women out here traveling. I meet them in every city with all aged kids, and I think it's important for women to hear that. We're out here and we're safe. Sometimes we pay too much for something. Sometimes we're unhappy with the taxi driver, but we're out here and we're making it, and we're fine. I think most of us feel like we're leading better lives than we would be in the US. So I'd like to encourage women and single mothers and families to really consider it an option."

Essential Travel Items

Really good backpacks. The more the kids can carry, the better, and we pare down to essential items, like chargers, a pair of flipflops and a good pair of trainers.

Chapter 9

Make a Plan for Your Stuff

This chapter assumes you have a lot of stuff. You might own a home, or you might be renting. Regardless, all of it needs to be dealt with when planning a month or a year on the road. God knows you shouldn't – and can't – take all that crap with you. One of the best tips I can give you right now is that less is more when it comes to packing. Take as little as you can. Then take less. If you don't have any stuff, then you've already reached the art of Zen, and I imagine you're a traveler. For most others, let me back up a minute.

We can't talk about stuff without talking about consumerism. The entire US economy, and much of our culture, is based on it. We're way past shopping for basic needs. Shopping has become our economic pride, our emotional support and our out-of-control addiction. Remember George W. Bush's post 9/11 directive for Americans to "go about their business" and "shop?" That was his way of demonstrating to terrorists that Americans could not be defeated – our victorious stand would be taken in the malls of the country.

(If you haven't seen George Carlin's brilliant stand-up skit on STUFF, go watch it now. Seriously, go do it. You can also watch Annie Leonard's Story of Stuff (storyofstuff.org), which shows how this obsession is literally killing us – and is, by the way, a fantastic Worldschooling resource. Her new series is on plastic. Watch that too.)

Of course many travelers are still quite attached to their stuff. But what travelers perhaps see more clearly than others is how burdensome and indulgent consumerism can be. There's nothing like hauling a suitcase around the world to show you how little you actually need.

No matter how much or how little we own, we have to make decisions about what to do with it before we head out. Many people I met on the road said they had a calling. When the inspiration took hold, they sold everything and hit the road. I am not one of those people. The very thought of selling my home sends cold shivers down my back. I'm a single mom who has spent most of my professional journalistic life working freelance. Not having anything to fall back on is simply not my style. I need *some* security. Right now, that security comes from having a home that I know I can rent while I am away, return to when I so choose, and count on in my later years. It also gives me comfort to know my son will have an asset in the event anything should happen to me. I believe in freedom and spontaneity as much as the next person, but also in making choices to create future security.

Other people feel differently.

One of my favorite message board conversations among traveling families raised this question of how to deal with personal belongings before hitting the road. Did people keep a home base? Did they own rental properties that supported them along the way? Or did they throw a Hail Mary and sell everything without looking back? If they *did* throw the Hail Mary, did they harbor regrets in retrospect?

There was a wide range of responses. A lot of people maintained a home base, either keeping their home empty or renting it out for income while on the road. Some families kept other rentals purely for income but had given up their primary homes; others sold their homes and put everything in storage. Still others sold everything and left their home country with a clean slate. Amazingly, these were the people who noted almost without exception that they had no regrets! "Best decision of my life," wrote one. "Never looked back," wrote another.

The one exception was a woman responding to the question of whether people feared they wouldn't be able to buy back into the place they had left – particularly in popular and gentrifying areas, like my own hometown in Santa Fe, New Mexico. "I do wonder if I'd be able to buy back in. But what's done is done," she wrote from Southeast Asia. I was struck by the relief — expressed almost with euphoria — from those who let go of everything and jumped into their travels with both feet. Again, that person is not me.

I'm someone who likes security, or at least the illusion of security, which I know is an irony considering my background is in reporting on wars and their repercussions. Or maybe that's the root of it — even in the most unstable of conflict situations, I always knew I had a home to return to. During these journalistic forays, and later as I traveled for pleasure, I rented out my house while traveling thousands of miles away, and rarely with any difficulties. As a young, single woman traveling, my costs were low, and I needed few creature comforts. Then I got older and I became a mother, and my body started to creak. Rather than enduring those

$2 hostels with stains on the mattress, I was willing to cut my trip short in order to afford a fancier hotel with 100 percent cotton sheets or an infinity pool. I began to want luxury, or at least some version of that that I could afford. I still felt confident that when the trip was over that I could go back home to what was comfortable and known, even if it was not necessarily where I wanted to live permanently.

In general, if you are unsure whether a longer-term adventure is for you, I'd suggest taking smaller steps, and renting out your home before selling everything. Yes, many have suggested that this strategy can weigh you down and limit your adventuring possibilities. It all depends on what you own and what level of security you feel you need. One day I hope to write that I sold everything and it was the best decision I ever made. I'm just not there yet. Plus, I wonder how well I'd manage the cash of a home sale. Five Star hotels, here I come?

*

If you've never heard the term "house hacking," you should embrace it here, particularly if you have no desire to sell your home. House hacking is a fancy word for creative use of a home that partially or entirely pays for your rent or mortgage. For example, when I am in the United States, I often rent my upstairs bedroom to help offset my mortgage. When I travel, I rent out the entire house. I wouldn't be able to afford travel otherwise.

If you're a renter, your choices are different. You might simply give up a lease, unless you are particularly attached to a place or school district and intend to return. If you want to keep your rental home, a landlord must OK a sublease. If a sublease is forbidden, you'll have to consider, and budget for, the cost of storing your belongings. Maybe you have a friend or family member with some extra room in their basement. Some families I met rented out their extra rooms in their large house, while others with greater means left their home empty, with friends or family occasionally checking in.

If you own your home and renting is on the agenda, you'll have to decide whether to hire a property manager, or manage it all yourself. Just be aware, property managers can charge up to 20%. It might be worth the peace of mind, but it does cut into your bottom line. I chose to manage my property myself, but with a dependable, long-term renter. Yes, there was that memorable week of trying to replace a malfunctioning composting toilet while I navigated the jungles of Ecuador... still, no regrets.

If you can find a way to have other people pay for your rent or mortgage at home while you're traveling (i.e. house hack), then you're in great shape. Even more so if you can make a profit. Because, with the exception of Western Europe, most apartments and houses around the world will have lower rents than in the US. In my case, I actually saved money by traveling and renting out my house. This is a concept that is difficult for many people to understand, but it's how many travelers are able to put together a life abroad. So rather than thinking of your mortgage as a barrier to travel – as many have explained to me – I recommend using your home as leverage. Let it be a key to your adventure and not a limiting factor.

Chapter 10

Get Your Documents in Order

Years ago, when I was more spontaneous and less informed, I bought a plane ticket to Brazil. I was going to meet my then boyfriend, whom I mentioned in Chapter 1, as he rode his motorcycle down the coast of South America. It was all very romantic.

I arrived at the ticket counter in Albuquerque dressed in my motorcycle gear and with only a small knapsack of toiletries, shorts, and some underwear.

"Where is your visa?" the airline counter person asked me. "What visa? Don't I get it on arrival?" This had been my experience in the past, but for whatever reason, the United States had decided to impose strict entry requirements on friendly nations like Brazil. Unbeknownst to me Brazil had in turn imposed the same strict requirements on Americans.

"No, you need a visa," the counter person repeated.

"But...how long does that take?" I asked, panic stricken.

"Up to three months if you apply today."

Three months wouldn't work. My boyfriend wouldn't be in Brazil anymore. Our relationship might be over by then! What's more, I had paid $600 for a non-refundable plane ticket. I quickly searched my mind for options. Then it hit me. I was in the very fortunate position of having two passports.

"What about French citizens? Do they need a visa?"

She checked her computer. "No."

I got out my credit card, paid an additional $900 for a ticket that left the following morning, drove an hour home, and grabbed my French passport. The next morning I returned for my flight to Brazil – as a French citizen.

This is not something you should count on doing. Because I am a dual citizen I was able to take this trip, though my ignorance and lack of preparation cost me quite a bit. This was one expensive mistake.

You may not have to apply for visas in advance for every country, but you most certainly need a valid passport to travel. Every member of your family will need one, even little Betty the baby who can't even sit up for a proper passport photo. A US passport gives you entry to most, though not all, countries in the world, with far fewer bureaucratic hoops than our foreign friends encounter visiting the US.

You can apply for a passport at a post office branch, or at other passport locations that you can find online. To renew a passport, you can usually apply directly online through travel.state.gov. Application costs vary, with extra fees for expedited service. Be sure to check all requirements, including the sometimes very specific passport photo parameters. In other words, no selfies!

To find specific information, including up to date costs, go to travel.state.gov

You can avoid expensive mistakes like the one I made by informing yourself of a country's rules well in advance. Visa requirements vary from country to country so be sure to research the current requirements in time to apply for any visas if needed.

Whether or not a formal visa is required, the length of stay in any given country is no joke. You may dream of staying in Europe for the next year, but unless you have a special visa or a European passport, you cannot stay more than three months in what's called the Schengen area. The name Schengen comes from the small Luxembourg town where the initial agreement was signed, and the area comprises 26 European countries that have agreed to abolish passport requirements for visitors traveling within their boundaries. Once you enter this zone you may travel freely within those countries during your stay allowance, which is 90 days in any 180-day period. There are some ways to extend that with certain work or student visas, but in general, keep in mind that you have three months within the zone for every 180 days. For many long-term travelers, that's not a lot of time.

In addition, from 2023 onward (at this writing), citizens of the US and over 60 other countries will need an electronic travel authorization to visit much of Europe. Any traveler to the Schengen zone will have to register with a European Travel Information and Authorization System (ETIAS). Some countries will also require visas. For more information go to: schengenvisainfo.com

There is an agreement similar to Schengen in Central America called the Central America-4 border agreement.

It includes Guatemala, El Salvador, Honduras, and Nicaragua, and allows visitors a 90-day visa to enter or pass through all of the above-listed countries without having to obtain additional permits.

Individual countries will have different requirements. Mexico once automatically granted a six-month stay upon arrival at the airport or port of entry, but that is no longer the case. The amount of time offered to tourists heading to Mexico sometimes appears arbitrary, based on return tickets or the whim of the immigration agent. Many speculate that Mexican officials got tired of foreign residents simply crossing the border every six months to avoid the resident visa process altogether. Regardless the reasoning, you (and your car if you are driving) will have to leave Mexico before the number of days on your visa expires. Visitors wanting to live for a prolonged time in Mexico should apply for a temporary resident visa (initial application is outside of Mexico), good for up to three years, or a permanent visa for those who have found their long-term home.

Many Asian countries allow visits for up to 90 days every half year.

The critical point is that these rules keep changing. Be sure to take the time to research the most up-to-date travel requirements of each country you'd like to visit.

Other important documents:

If you are a single parent, you may need permission from the other parent or legal guardian to travel out of state – a travel consent letter. Travel consent letters vary but generally include: Who is traveling with the child; contact information of legal guardians; permission outlining specific details of where the child will be going (out of state? out of country?); and for which dates. This letter should be signed by both parents in front of a notary. Some countries belonging to the Hague Convention require the document be apostilled, meaning the document is certified for use in another country. Be sure to check on requirements before leaving.

If you are divorced, such travel requirements should be included in a custody order. That order may state that no permission is needed, or it might be more strict and require a parental permission for each out-of-state or international trip. Be aware of any legal documents you might need to travel with your minor children, especially if they have a different last name. For many years, I carried a copy of my son's birth certificate with me, which did not list anyone's name but mine as a parent, so I avoided having to present any letters of permission.

As a single parent I also carry a power of attorney, guardianship documents should anything happen to me, and my will. More on this in the chapter on single parent travel, but these documents are good for anyone to have. There are free samples on sites like nolo.com or rocketlawyer.com.

Vaccinations

During the COVID-19 crisis many people became so focused on the virus and its vaccination requirements, that they forgot all about other required vaccinations. For example, a yellow fever vaccination is required to enter many countries in Africa. Contact a travel center or infectious disease specialist to find out what you need for more exotic travel locales, and always check various government sites for ever-changing regulations. It's also useful to ask fellow travelers what might be suggested, even if not required. For example, while not required, a rabies vaccine is highly recommended in many Asian countries where both monkey and dog bites are common. Even if the puncture is mild you can get rabies, which has no cure.

Let me tell you how I learned this information.

My son and I have received many vaccines to travel. But when, shortly before our trip to Cambodia, an infectious disease doctor also suggested I get a rabies shot, I declined. Rabies was not my concern.

Weeks later, while visiting remote villages on the Cambodian border, a man in a small café motioned for Aiden to come look at something. There in a cardboard box was a mother dog and her just born crew of little pups. He peered into the box then looked at me, overjoyed. I joined him and leaned over the edge of the box for a better view. Suddenly I felt a set of teeth in my behind, some yelling and the screech of a dog as the owner kicked this mutt out of the way. It happened fast — a protective response by this papa dog toward his pups. His small teeth cut through my pants and punctured my skin.

The café owner was mortified. "He's never seen a white person before. I'm so sorry."

I didn't think much about it and we went about our day. That night over noodle soup with friends who worked in the region, I conveyed the story, giggling at this racist mutt and his protective nature.

"Wait, what did you say? The dog punctured your skin!?"

"Just a tiny bit. It hurt in the moment, but it's ok."

One of the guys launched into a tirade about how rabies is 100 percent fatal if not treated within 24 hours, and didn't I know how serious this was? I obviously had no idea how serious it was or I wouldn't have been sitting there enjoying my soup. Others seated at the table were equally surprised by the dramatic response. We understood quickly that my friend was not joking. I could see fear on his face, which sent my heart racing. Now I was scared too.

"We're going to the hospital RIGHT NOW!" my friend yelled.

He literally pulled me out of my seat, threw some money on the table next to my abandoned soup, and led us to the car. We packed into his vehicle and bolted for the hospital, which was practically deserted. It was an expensive foreign hospital, beautiful and clean, with new equipment and nurses in crisp uniforms. My friend breathlessly explained the situation to the administrator, and we were ushered into a room where I began to receive the first of a series of preventative injections for rabies. The nurse reiterated in a calm voice the danger of rabies if not treated within 24 hours.

This was the first of seven shots injected into my stomach that I would receive over the next few months. I was just glad I was the one bitten, and not Aiden. I had been uneducated and careless, and now I was paying the price.

Now you know too: bites from rabid dogs are common in Asian countries, and bites from monkeys even more so. A rabies shot is a good bet if you're planning on staying for a while, and especially if you have kids who love seeing wild or wandering animals and feel the desire to interact with them (which they should never do, by the way. Just saying).

One afternote: it took an immense amount of bureaucratic back and forth but my travel insurance paid for the many months of injections my treatment required. I was grateful for that, too.

LAUNCH

We arrived in San Miguel de Allende,
Mexico, one year after my mother's death.
It was the beginning of our new life.
Joining us was my dear friend Wanda.

Chapter 11

What Happens
When We Get There?

Traditional Lodging

Once you've decided that you're really going to go —
congratulations! — you can start exploring where
you're going, how you're going to get there, and what
your options are for accommodation. Much of this will
depend on your length of stay. Are you passing through
and looking for comfort? Do you need a month-long
rental with amenities to cook for your family? Are you
used to nice hotels — maybe all-inclusive resorts? —
or do you prefer bare-bones campsites on the outskirts
of town?

Regardless of what you choose, lodging will likely be
the next biggest ticket item after airfare, so be sure
to research the options, especially if you're traveling
for a long time. One strategy I recommend, especially
if you are unsure of an area, is to start by reserving a
nice hotel room for the first day or two after arrival. If
you've had a long flight and the kids are cranky, it helps

everyone adjust and get their bearings. The comfort of a dependable landing spot from which to begin your exploration will be worth the extra price. When possible, I also reserve a taxi from the airport to avoid haggling right off the airplane. If you have flown internationally, you're likely familiar with the barrage of hawkers and hagglers who descend upon newly-arrived, under-slept travelers who may not yet understand proper pricing. A taxi driver may float an exorbitant rate to your hotel just to see if you're paying attention. With new and confusing currency, you could end up spending a few days budget on a single ride.

If you haven't already reserved a hotel, you'll have to find a place for the night. Traditional hotels might be the most expensive housing option, but they can also be convenient, for example if the hotel is near the airport and you have an early flight. Booking.com, expedia.com, VRBO.com, or hoteltonight.com can offer good deals on last minute stays.

There are lots of lower-cost and even no-cost options as well, and this chapter explores some of these. I don't know about you, but my 'I'll sleep on the bow of a boat to save the costs of a bed' days are over. But I'm still very engaged in trying to lower costs wherever possible.

Let's start with some of the most popular options:

Airbnb and VRBO are among the most popular choices for families, primarily because of kitchen availability. For large families especially, having your own kitchen saves time and money. Being able to cook your own food also helps calm finicky and possibly nervous new travelers who yearn for what they ate back home. If you plan to stay a while, always reach out and ask if there might be a better rate. People are often open to negotiating for longer stays.

Hostels have come a long way. Many have graduated from only offering a few stringy hammocks and rooms packed with bunk beds, to now much more comfortable single rooms, and even family rooms. Hostels are great not only for the lower costs and access to a kitchen, but for the chance to mingle with other travelers. (That said, our last hostel is where my young son was first introduced to the adult and X-rated game, Cards Against Humanity, so there's that.)

For single or smaller family-unit travelers, or those who want more social connection, hostels are a great choice — and they're often located in prime locations for city exploration. My son and I have had great hostel experiences. However, and contrary to popular belief, some can be quite expensive, and others may not accept children. Many now have beautiful upgrades, and you can usually find one with a private bathroom. I've always chosen private rooms with a door that locked. Some also include amazing breakfasts, such as one lodge we stayed in in the Colombian hills. I'm not sure I've ever tasted such wonderful coffee...

Alternative Accommodation Options

There are plenty of options to help lower the cost of accommodations. Believe it or not, some of these options are free — or pretty darn close.

There are several home exchange and home rental groups on Facebook, and some specifically for World-schoolers. Try World School House Swap/Sit/Rent on Facebook or People Like Us (peoplelikeus.world) with international home exchanges, homes listed on craigslist.com, or boundless.life, which offers "turnkey" homes with good WiFi as working hubs for remote families. Even couchsurfing.com provides more options these days. Plus, these groups have occasional or regular Meetups so you can get a sense ahead of time of the people offering their homes.

It simply takes a lot of resourcefulness and creativity. With these two elements in hand, the opportunities can open for you, whether your goal is to deeply engage with a community, educate yourself, or create special experiences for you and your children. Below I detail some of the most popular options families have chosen to save money on accommodation.

Housesitting

Trustedhousesitters.com was one of my most cherished finds during our years of travel. This website allows you to search the world over for people needing house sitters and those eager to housesit, sometimes for a long weekend, sometimes for a season. Usually it requires care of pets, sometimes many (see the interview with Karen King and family). If your children miss their pets, this can be a great gift. Some homes even come with cars and most homeowners are happy to leave an information packet to help you adjust to the home and the town. There is an application process, and for popular locations, beautiful homes and longer stays, the competition can be fierce. The annual fee can be reduced if you bring others to the trustedhousesitters.com site. Regardless, the amount easily pays for itself with just a few nights lodging in a high cost of living area.

Once you're a member, you can also list your own properties and pets. I've frequently posted my home and the care of my dear dogs when I've had to leave town. I appreciate the free and vetted house sitters I've chosen so far, many of whom remain good friends to this day.

Home Exchange

Homeexchange.com is another popular option for international home exchanges, with an annual membership required. Lovehomeswap.com offers holiday homes to exchange, also with a membership fee. There are any number of additional Facebook groups offering house swapping in locations around the world, plus female travel boards, and those for single women and moms. Always be careful and check with others about their experience. Use verified sites and sources before staying anywhere.

Volunteer Opportunities or Work Exchanges

There are travel experiences, including a myriad of volunteer programs, that offer housing. But please approach volunteer opportunities with caution! There are scams, poorly organized programs, and opportunities that can be morally questionable.

For example, you may feel the desire to work with orphans in a particular country. It's warm and fuzzy and the optics are great for your Instagram account. Yet psychologists have repeatedly warned that such short-term volunteerism, while possibly good for the volunteer, can have lasting negative impacts on a child already challenged with attachment issues.

The same goes for programs dealing with wildlife. Want to ride an elephant? Did you know that elephants are brutally beaten in order to get them used to carrying tourists? The more you know, the more depressing it can get. But it's important to know. We don't simply want a world of travelers; we want responsible people and families exploring other cultures with respect and care. If volunteerism is what you're looking for, make sure that any program is safe, reputable, and well-organized. There are so many opportunities to help organizations that are doing wonderful work. The one you choose should benefit the community or animals as much as or more than it benefits you and your family. Volunteerforever.com has a list of the best international volunteer programs, organizations and projects, with additional volunteer guides for doctors, nurses, and teens. It named goeco.org and viavolunteers.com as some of the most ethical volunteer programs.

Always have direct contact with someone at the host organization, read the reviews, and ask other travelers who've been through the programs.

Many families have had great experiences WWOOFing (wwoof.net). That's World Wide Opportunities on Organic Farms. Each experience is different, and the work is not often easy, but room and board are provided and many volunteers have raved about the experiences. Check out their info page to see if it's suitable for children. See my interview with Jesica Sweedler DeHart in the coming pages.

Workaway.info offers cultural exchange, working holidays and volunteerism in 170 countries. In exchange for a certain number of work hours (which differs depending on the host) the participant is offered room and board. The fees are marked on their website and the variety of projects and locations is immense. You can also be a Workaway host, which is a good way to stay connected to the traveling community once you're done traveling.

Some of the more institutional options include the Peace Corps, which provides intensive language training and pay, but is open only to US citizens. There's Volunteer Service Overseas and UN Volunteers (vsointernational.org and unv.org), which usually don't require any fees and may cover your expenses, even offering a small stipend. There are kibbutzim in Israel (kibbutzvolunteer.com) or conservation volunteers in Australia or New Zealand (conservationvolunteers.com.au), with opportunities for beach clean up or repairing damaged lands after floods or fire. Some of these require a fee to participate, but do provide room and board.

The above mentioned are just a small taste of some of the opportunities available to traveling families. A quick Google search will bring up countless others, many asking for a weekly or monthly fee. A fee is not an indication of a dubious project; often the fees are going to a good cause. If cost is a factor in your desire to travel, or you want a deeper experience of a place, working and volunteering can be a good choice for your family. Never forget to reach out to other online communities for feedback and suggestions. The ones who have been there can often pave your way.

Jesica Sweedler Dehart

WWOOfing through Europe

"It was the best year of our entire lives. It wasn't easy but it was worth it 100%. WWOOFing became an absolute vacation for me from all of that planning."

For many years Jesica had envisioned a year abroad, exposing her two sons to different cultures, ways of living, and foods. She wanted her kids to become global citizens with the ability to navigate a fast-changing world. Since her husband Dennis was a college art professor, they knew he would have regular sabbaticals. The beauty of a sabbatical, which generally is six months to a year's leave for the purpose of professional reflection and rejuvenation (often for the purpose of writing a book) is that generally it is paid, either in full or in part.

As the sabbatical year approached, they started planning their travel. Dennis would receive 75% of his salary, and the couple had saved an additional $10,000.

They also rented out their primary and secondary homes in the Pacific Northwest of the United States. This covered their home expenses plus a bit more. Next, they had to pay for the actual travel, and for a family of four the costs can be high. Enter WWOOF-ing. Worldwide Opportunities on Organic Farms is an opportunity to receive room and board at locations in every corner of the world in exchange for work. This work can take the form of physical labor — these are farms, after all — but also include a range of other jobs, including baking, photography, or helping families plan and organize their businesses. For Jesica's family, WWOOFing became the biggest savings of their trip.

"I calculated that for every week in Europe that we WWOOFed, we saved at least a minimum of $1,000 if not $1500 from what we had budgeted. Especially because in many places, when you have four people traveling it requires two rooms."

Overall, the family spent six weeks WWOOFing in Europe, where they knew living expenses would be most costly.

Here's how the process works: The site wwoof.net (or wwoofusa.org for US options) allows you to see basic descriptions of the farms and submit an application.

Once you pay a basic membership fee you can contact people directly. You can see which stays might take four people, or which locations take children (many do not). Some take people only in the summer, others want a six-month commitment.

"The moment you put in that you have two kids, you really scale it back significantly, because anybody that's going to take a family with two kids, in my experience, had far lower expectations of the amount of work that will be completed."

In their application, they noted that Dennis was a professional photographer willing to offer photoshoots, and that Jesica loved to bake and cook and was skilled at canning fruit and vegetables. Dennis' skills ended up being popular, and he provided photo shoots for many of the farms where they stayed. They also indicated other needs. For example, they wanted sheets and blankets, as they didn't have sleeping bags, and they preferred to stay where there were other WWOOFers. They wanted to be where they could get easily into town or access a train or bus.

Jesica suggests you choose locations based on interest and send letters of introduction. And know that there can be last-minute changes. When one farm cancelled on them at the last minute — they withdrew the work exchange in order to rent out the room for top dollar during the high season — they were able to contact the country liaison (each country has one) and get reassigned.

Traditionally while WWOOFing, meals are eaten family style at least for lunch and dinner. All food is provided for you. But some homeowners can be particular — at one luxurious location they weren't allowed to eat with the owners, and were simply refunded the amount of their groceries.

Also, be careful what boxes you tick on your application, and be sure to note only the tasks and skills that you are really willing to do. Don't over-represent yourself, she warns, or you may be expected to do far more than you'd like. Jesica's best experiences followed email or phone communication ahead of time, spelling out arrangements and expectations very specifically. Each host will expect a given number of days and number of hours within those days. Be sure you understand what is expected — and if the host isn't good about communicating it's probably best to move on.

"We definitely didn't pick the ones where you were expected to work six days a week and eight hours a day. We skipped those and did the more lenient, leisurely ones."

The family learned little things, like not to over indulge in fresh olive oil that a family offers (because it can be scarce and difficult to produce), and that one should only heat as much water as is needed to avoid wasting precious gas. They also discovered new skills. "The boys learned that they were amazing challah bakers, and that if they could sell that to a host then that could be their job for the day."

Their best WWOOFing experiences have led to lifelong friendships. In Bilbao, Spain, for example, they had to remind the family that they were there to work. "We took walks and went hiking, hung out by a river, crafted, and cooked meals together. It felt more like a culture exchange."

"Even though my family didn't love WWOOFing as much as I did, I loved it because that was my biggest vacation. It was a lot of work for me just figuring out where we were sleeping, eating, and how we were getting from place to place. WWOOFing became an absolute vacation for me from all of that planning."

Jesica, whose family is Jewish, described Israel as an "incredible experience. It was our first time being in a country where we felt total belonging. We were there over Hanukkah, and just to be centered religiously, culturally, in a country experience, was a real feeling of belonging."

For Jesica, it meant learning more about her own family's history in Israel, plus aspects of her religion she knew little about. For example, she was surprised to find that 50% of Israeli Jews are Jews of color, unlike in the United States where the number hovers closer to 10%.

"I knew all about the Ethiopian Jews. I knew all about the Sephardic Jews and Ashkenazi Jews, but I didn't really understand Mizrahi Jews. That was a new term for me. What I saw in Israel was that being Jewish is not a white-dominant thing like in the US because of the way the diaspora happened. Ashkenazi Jews, predominantly, and Sephardic Jews came to the US, but Jews of color went more to Israel, including those from the diaspora who fled to Africa. It was eye opening, and a gift to realize how diverse my Judaism is."

When Jesica returned home she changed her social media feed to follow Mizrahi Jews and many Jews of color, because "I realized that is so much more reflective of Israel," she said.

The family had loosely structured their trip around artist residencies Dennis had scheduled in various countries: Malaysia, Thailand, Portugal and the Netherlands, plus a teaching gig in Dubai. Between residencies, they planned a mixture of "fun travel" with a break from homeschooling. Regardless of the location, travel days — whether by train, plane or bus or boat — were always the most expensive, and nerve-wracking.

"Those were the days we lost it, people cried, there were tantrums with kids carrying their backpacks."

Other challenges for Jesica revolved around her health. Traveling the world with celiac disease (an autoimmune reaction to gluten) and IBS made it hard for her to eat and maintain a healthy weight.

Amazingly, the family chose to travel without phones. Though she says she has no regrets, Jesica admits that the world is no longer set up for those traveling without them.

Big cities were especially difficult with young children, whereas smaller towns with more space were easier to navigate. The Netherlands was great for its walking and biking, giving the kids freedom and independence they couldn't have in other cities. In Southeast Asia they scheduled visits to schools, for a day or an afternoon, which gave them perspective on their own school experiences.

One lesson was on timing. Having three or four weeks or a month where you don't go anywhere was critical, she said. "If we could do it all over again, we'd take it slower and stay longer in favorite locations."

"I feel like travel changed us both as individuals but also very much as a family," Jesica said. "My kids and especially my older teen had such over-inflated views of how great America is. I think he really came to appreciate what he has, but also was humbled by how much the US could learn from other countries as well. They really learned the meaning of 'first world problems' on this trip."

Essential Travel Items

This was our first time traveling with iPads, and since we didn't have phones, using maps.me (which is downloadable and can be used without data) was a lifesaver.

We are huge readers so the kids relied heavily on OverDrive and had set up library accounts with multiple libraries. They were able to download endless books and audiobooks that kept them satiated. We still bought them physical books when we came across English language bookstores but the audiobooks and constant access to things to read kept them very happy.

We also let them each bring a bag of LEGOs, and that bag grew considerably during our travels. But it was the toy that gave them so much joy and really kept them happy.

My husband would say his electric shaver was essential. He really liked keeping his hair trimmed in South East Asia where it got quite hot. We also brought Neutrogena 70 SPF sunscreen, which kept the two that easily burn well protected.

Compression packing cubes were also a plus.

Chapter 12

Slow Down

You're finally leaving the country — maybe for the first time. You may feel so excited to finally begin traveling that you want to tick off every bucket item in the span of a year. One hundred and ninety-seven countries in one year? Let's go for it! YOLO!

I would strongly warn against this. Fast travel can destroy your — and especially your child's — interest in travel for good. In this case less is so much more.

Fast travel — e.g. ten countries in ten days — is exhausting, and most often the traveler gains little or nothing from the experience. It eats your budget — it costs more because you're always eating out, and there are few deals on accommodations when your stay is so brief. It also eats your energy, all of which is put into organizing and scheduling, with almost no downtime. By the time you return home you'll need a vacation from your vacation.

Slow travel, on the other hand, takes you to fewer places in a given amount of time. But you spend more time in each place, getting to know an area and its people. Children often acclimate better, and your travel costs, whether by ground or air, are lower. Longer stays also allow families to negotiate lower lodging costs, and if you have a kitchen, you spend time in local markets and then cook for yourselves. For larger families especially, there are myriad benefits of being able to cook at home.

A word about food: For me and so many others, learning about regional food is one of the best parts of travel. I advise any family to also take time to discover local markets and local cuisine. There are few things as exciting or memorable for children than seeing *cuy* (guinea pig) on a stick in Peru, vats of fried grasshoppers in Mexico, the meat markets of southern France, or the night markets of Southeast Asia.

The extraordinary traveler, chef, and food writer Anthony Bourdain once said, "Food is everything we are. It's an extension of nationalist feeling, ethnic feeling, your personal history, your province, your region, your tribe, your grandma. It's inseparable from those from the get-go."

With slow travel the point is to take your time and to absorb as much of the culture you are visiting as you can. You may visit only three places in the span of a year, instead of 20. But your children — and your central nervous system — will thank you.

Jay Shapiro

Challenging What is "Normal"

"AND not OR, you can have both. It's absolutely possible."

Many families you meet on the road will amaze you. Once you get out in the world you encounter people with astonishing abilities. They not only travel through a vast number of countries while doing incredibly creative start-up work, but they help other travelers, sharing endless hacks, while also placing the highest value on family and parenting. Jay is one of those travelers.

Jay is a tech guy, creating apps and most recently launching a gaming center in Nairobi, Kenya, called Usiku, where Africans are creating games with the larger goal of harnessing the power of gamification for positive social impact in communities. Usiku (<u>usiku.</u><u>games</u>) was born after years of world travel with his two kids, Kurt and Maya, and his wife Alice — another powerhouse who runs a nonprofit accelerator helping outfits like the World Bank.

The Canadian family has always traveled, so Jay's kids haven't known anything else, he said. They took their son to Melbourne, Australia, when he was only a few months old; their daughter was in India when she was still under a year, riding in backpacks as they toured the country.

"I'm a big believer that normal is just what you know," he said.

A lot of their travel was done in a large recreational vehicle Jay called the Eco Roamer. This allowed them to venture to a new place every day, whether it was a glacier in Alaska or some desert or forest, while providing a consistency of place for the kids.

"At night the kids would go back to their beds with their stuffed animals, their pillows, and us. That provided the consistency, that stability, that is the anchor in their lives, and that gives us a lot of latitude to cover a lot of latitude."

They'd park the Eco Roamer when they traveled overseas. His teen son spent time in Greece with World-school guru Lainie Liberti (projectworldschool.com).

They spent a month in Italy as a family, another month in Singapore, then Thailand, Cambodia, and Mexico. They stayed in Mexico for several weeks before heading back to their home in New Jersey. After three weeks of rest, they set off again, this time to Nairobi, Cape Town, and Bangalore. Every year in the summer months, they go to Canada to spend time with family.

Not everyone has the capacity for such extensive traveling, at least not right out the gate. But Jay's advice to mere mortals is simple: do it.

"I say start. The second thing is 'don't wait.' I think a lot of people think 'some day I'm going to retire' or 'I'm just going to make enough money to do that.' And either 'some day' never comes, or by that point you're too old. Your life is now, so live it." Now more than ever, there are ways to have your career *and* travel. It used to be a choice; now you can have both, he said.

"Our family sort of motto — and we were going to get a tattoo someday — is 'AND not OR.' You can have both, it's absolutely possible. So many people's jobs are now becoming virtualized, or they're working in co-working spaces where they don't even realize they're location independent already."

The first step is the hardest. Jay likened it to a huge boulder that at first seems impossible to budge. Once it begins to roll the momentum keeps it moving. Similarly, once you finally convince yourself that you are going to start traveling, everything else kind of flows, Jay said, adding that these days these are so many online tools and hacks available to travelers. Jay uses a mail service for his snail mail that goes through an electronic box and gets scanned. He takes a look at his app each day then decides which letters get shredded, which gets kept, and which gets forwarded. "It's really easy."

He takes the same easy approach to educating his kids, for example during a recent trip to Cambodia.

"I've been going to Cambodia for decades and I love it as a country. The people are beautiful, the country is beautiful, the story is tragic, the history is amazing." He said it was the perfect Worldschooling location, particularly the ruins of Angkor Wat. "As a ten- and a twelve-year-old, they got to climb over the rocks and through these tunnels and dark, scary rooms and look at the roots. It's just fantasmical to do it. I wish I had seen it when I was ten."

After exploring the physical site, his son followed up with a research project on the Khmer Kingdom and its history, archaeology and architecture. He turned it into a multi-week multidisciplinary research project that was grounded in a tactile experience he will never forget.

In Venice, Italy, the family walked through the Jewish ghetto, a place that affected them deeply. "Particularly if you're twelve, because they're just starting to understand what it all means. To be able to be there and to literally see the gates, will make it more real for them than any history class ever could... My favorite part is just giving them those experiences."

That said, Jay is not a radical unschooler. He incorporates a curiosity-based approach when possible, while also adhering to traditional math and science classes. The family uses a platform called IXL to follow the full New Jersey curriculum. At the end of the year Jay's kids will be at the same level as their peers, and probably beyond. Jay and his wife both hold master's degrees, and they expect their children also will attend university or college.

"But they will go to it for a very different reason than we did," he said. "They're going to graduate into a very different world than we did."

Jay studied computer science then got an MBA in order to further his career. But in 20 or 30 years the jobs he had may not exist, he said. So much is being automated through artificial intelligence, (which also happens to be Jay's new field), that vocational training for those jobs is going to be irrelevant.

"Instead, we're going back to first principles, the classic liberal arts education of studying philosophy and history and art. This is so they can exist as better humans in that world that doesn't quite exist yet, and that's why they're going to go to college and university."

His final words of advice to tentative travelers are this: "If you are in the US, start in the US. There's a whole lot to see and it's easy, because you don't have to worry about visas and insurance, shots and currencies. I absolutely encourage people to travel around the world. We've been in dozens and dozens of countries. But if you're scared, just go take a short trip. If you're in the Southwest, go to Canyon De Chelly in Arizona; if you're in the Northwest, go to Vancouver and Vancouver Island. Wherever you are, I guarantee you there's somewhere gorgeous nearby with people who you've never met, who are nicer than you can imagine."

Essential Travel Items

Tripit.com is an app and a tool that makes travel, particularly with the family, much easier. It tracks your flights, your changes, and the maps of the airport where you have to run to get the next connection. It also tracks all your loyalty points, so it makes travel days, which are the most stressful part of traveling, less stressful.

The second one is a practice, where every night at dinner as a family, wherever we may be, and wherever dinner is, whatever shape that might take, whether it's the kitchen table or a taco stand in Guanajuato, we do what we call our 'thankful fors.' What happened today that you're thankful for? We do that every night, adults and kids together. It encourages a mindfulness about your day, and reminds us and them the importance of being grateful. It teaches them an attitude of gratitude.

The third one is that we can't travel if we can't work. If I was at home, I'd be in an office working. I'd rather be working in Bali under a palapa looking at a rice field, than in a cubicle. People say, 'you're in Bali, how can you be working?' Well, because that's what pays for Kurt and Maya. So just be okay with that need to work, and make space for that. Then of course having some form of connectivity to be able to do that is critical.

Chapter 13

Locate Your Tribe

One beautiful thing about traveling communities is that our numbers just keep growing. There are resources that exist now that did not exist even a year ago, including blog sites, podcasts, Facebook pages, conferences and organized travel groups and events. It's easier than ever to reach out to people before you leave — and certainly to reach out while you're on the road, especially if you've just hit that three-month mark, which by many accounts is quite a hurdle.

A word of warning for those newly arrived in a new place: some settled expat families you meet may seem to be standoffish. You're not imagining it. Particularly in areas popular with tourists and expats, new families stream in and ask established families for all kinds of help. Then within days or weeks, they leave. You can understand a certain lack of excitement to entertain you during your stay. It's nothing personal; they're just not eager to put time and energy into a relationship that will likely end before it ever had a chance to grow.

Don't let this deter you. Almost every location you visit will have some sort of community center or forum for information, most directed precisely at expats. Larger areas will have a more developed list-serve. In San Miguel de Allende, Mexico, for example, there is a well-developed list-serv with members so active they're practically conversing in real time. Residents seek advice on doctors, restaurants, visas, or how to get dog pee out of their Persian rug (true story). For every question there is a patient and usually well-informed answer.

Online community

In addition to list-servs there is usually a location Facebook page. There most often are additional pages for expats, kids and families, single people, mothers, or food lovers. A Facebook search of your location can bring up groups, some of which you must "apply" to join. Join all that you can find, especially when you're just starting out. Remember that people are much more receptive to any questions if they see you've done a bit of research beforehand. For example, if you have a question, do a quick search on the Facebook page to see if it has been answered (twenty times) before.

Bookstores

Small towns sometimes have great bookstores, like Amate Books in downtown Oaxaca, Mexico, where foreigners congregate to exchange information. Oaxaca also has a great library with an English books section, advertised social events, and a newsletter. Often you can find an expat-run newspaper, though those are sometimes harder to locate than a Facebook page. In big cities you're likely to find plenty of bookstores where travelers congregate. Some of them are quite famous, like Shakespeare and Company on the banks of the Seine in Paris.

Parks

Parks and soccer fields should be at the top of your list when visiting any new location. There you can connect with families, and your kid can spend time outdoors. The people you meet may just be visiting, or they may have relocated years earlier and have a wealth of information they're willing to share.

Restaurants or cafes

On many occasions I have approached Americans or expat-looking families in restaurants and asked if they were residents. Without exception I got useful information, friendly advice, and sometimes even play dates. Most families understand the need to connect with others, and for their children to meet and interact. Even if they're only visiting, most people are usually open and happy to share what they've learned. I've spent many a day with other touring families and their kids — who were happy to have new friends, if only for a few days, or even hours. This is especially true for single parents traveling or parents traveling with only one child.

Schools

Local schools are another resource. I once reached out to a Waldorf school and asked if the director might share my name with parents willing to talk to me about their experiences. Several contacted me and provided lots of useful information. Another time we stopped at a local school to ask if we could borrow some English language young adult novels. This interaction ended up changing the trajectory of our travels. We came back every few days for another book (Aiden reads very quickly), made friends with the principal, and decided the following year to move to this town where my son would attend this school.

Which brings me back to slow travel. So many families I've interviewed refer to the importance of slow travel, and regret that they didn't do it. This is particularly important for children. Each child is different, but in general kids want and appreciate a sense of stability, even if they don't yet havethe vocabulary to express it. This isn't always easy to find on the road, but when you do, it makes for a richer experience with more connections.

After meeting a group of Worldschoolers in Mexico, we decided to make the country our home for several years.

Lydia Bradbury

Military Families

"Chaos is chaos so you might as well have a decent view and better food."

I met Lydia and her three kids, all under the age of five, on their first-ever international trip to Guanajuato, Mexico. Married to a US Marine, the 30-something woman was clearly used to moving with the military, and the family had often taken car trips up and down the east coast of the US. Now she was dipping her toe into international waters to see how the kids would manage on a longer trip, further from home.

The family lived on a military base in South Carolina, with plans to downsize and save money to one day afford another place overseas. "Our ultimate goal is to do three months home, three months gone. Whenever dad's available we'd be home," Lydia said. She always leaned toward homeschooling and unschooling, which is what brought her to a Worldschooling conference in Mexico in the first place. By connecting with like-minded families, she wanted to gain tips and tricks for the road. After her first week traveling, she had some tips of her own to share, and things she would definitely do differently next time.

"One crucial lesson is that the family needs to stop when it gets dark, not necessarily for safety, but for everybody's sanity. Everyone starts melting down and I'm tired at that point, so I don't handle things as well as I could if we had stopped previously," she said.

Keeping to her children's bedtime schedules was also important, as was letting go of the desire to see everything just because there's so much to see. "It's not worth seeing a museum at 7pm if everyone is having a breakdown. There's time for that." Another big lesson for a family with small children was having a kitchen. Not that children shouldn't be tasting new, local foods, but familiarity is comfort. When everything else in their surroundings has changed, food can be a constant. In fact, several families suggested bringing along a jar of peanut butter. It's difficult to find overseas, is often familiar to kids, and acts as quick protein, Lydia said.

"Everybody's sick of quesadillas; I will forever more do Airbnb or house rentals so I can have a kitchen."

Packing was also a challenge, and she admits to underpacking in some areas, overpacking in others. She needed way more underwear and socks and far fewer tops and pants. The miscalculation meant she was spending a lot of time doing laundry — or trying to. Adjusting to more flexible business hours was proving to be an additional challenge.

"You have to take into consideration the lifestyle and culture of Mexican time or Greek time. Those are very real things. So we've been re-wearing a lot."

I was surprised to hear that underpacking and tiring of quesadillas were Lydia's biggest challenges, considering she was a solo mom traveling with three small children. But she said raising kids on her own is familiar, since her military husband is gone much of the time.

"I don't feel like it's any more work traveling than it is at home, other than the packing," she jokes. Lydia is fortunate not only to have her husband's financial support, but also his full emotional support.

"He says, 'just go. You do it by yourself anyway, so if you want to do it somewhere nicer and cheaper, then go.' He knows I'm used to not having that help, so I might as well be somewhere with a view."

Both parents want their kids to be bilingual or even trilingual, and on their first trip the eldest was picking up Spanish fast. The child also found his tribe of adventuring friends; military children are incredibly resilient, but not all are as fearless, Lydia said.

"We kind of live in a protected Mayberry bubble on base, and we're the only people like us. By that I mean my kids climb higher and do scarier things, and I'm okay with it. Being with other Worldschoolers, we're surrounded by other people that are okay with it, too. For the first time in our lives, they feel like they're finally with their people."

Lydia acknowledges that many mothers get caught up on the fear of traveling alone and adds that "If you get caught up in the fear on the front end, you'll never go. Too many people get wrapped up in a location not being a first world country, or having crime, but they forget about all the crime going on the states. It happens all the time. I'm not afraid to go to a movie in Mexico, whereas in the states I might second guess it. That's a big thing. Everybody sent me emails concerned about my single-white-female-three-kids-safety in Mexico, and I haven't had an uncomfortable moment yet. That doesn't mean those moments are not there, and that you don't need to be aware of them. But getting caught up on what the media says is not how you get to the opportunity."

Essential Travel Items

Gum, gum, gum. And sticker books.

I made a point to download an app for audio books and storytelling because that's one thing I was afraid we would miss horribly. We have a huge book collection at home that makes up a bulk of our house. We made sure we had books.

We went out and found a LEGO-ish item to entertain the kids. We didn't pack any toys, except some small toy cars.

We packed our Daddy Dolls. That's a military thing. There's a military couple that created Daddy Dolls and you can buy them in 12-inch, 18-inch and full size, like toddler size. They have a picture of your husband in uniform on them. Each boy has a daddy doll with him, and that's been an important comfort item.

For voracious readers OverDrive's Libby app for libraries is absolutely essential. It works for all public libraries; you just enter your library card — you can have multiple library cards added — and you have access to thousands of books in a moment.

Chapter 14

Yes, there are Challenges when Traveling with Kids

My son one night during our third month of travel woke me in tears saying he was lonely, missed his dogs and friends (in that order), and wanted to go home. Immediately. With amazing clarity, he explained to me that when I was lonely or missed my friends, all I had to do was call them on my phone, send a text, or go to Facebook. He had no way to similarly connect. He was correct. At nine years old he had no computer, no phone, only limited time on his iPad, and limited Spanish skills to interact with local children. I couldn't believe how I had overlooked my very clear advantage. I felt selfish and uninformed. I just assumed he would follow me around the world and deal skillfully with the absence of his friends, schoolmates, and beloved dogs. Suddenly I saw how much he was struggling.

The next day we contacted friends at home and set up a multiplayer Minecraft game with our neighbor. We found a local animal shelter in the Mexican town we were visiting, where my son eventually signed up

to volunteer and became the dedicated puppy social-
izer. I also allowed him more computer time to make
up for his loneliness. I'd like to say that I forever after
remained sensitive to his needs and sadness, but there
are new challenges every day, and it takes a lot of sensitivity and communication to get through it. Just like
life. We eventually made it over this particular hump.
Then we hit the road again.

Next was a shorter visit to Colombia. After a week in
Medellin, I was pretty convinced I could live there forever. My son was not. "But mom, there are no kids my
age here! They're all babies or teenagers. There aren't
any ten-year-olds." Of course the statement was absurd, but for Aiden it was true. We hadn't met any other families, and since we were staying in the Poblado
district, known for high-end bars and cafes, partying
youngsters, and chic clothing stores, it was not the
most family-friendly environment. I chose the area because it was the safest for tourists, but it was not where
longer-term families might relocate. Plus, during our
daytime adventures, kids his age were in school.

The truth is that it takes time to get to know a place, and
a week is never enough time to get to a town's second
layer. That's the layer after a quick tourist visit, the one

you'll need to discover after museums, historic sites, or popular one-time tourist activities. A second, third and even fourth layer needs to be uncovered to comfortably stay longer in a place, or even to relocate. Without it, you haven't really "seen" a place.

In Medellin, for example, it took me a week just to learn about various Facebook groups, what schools existed, and which were best and why. We were already long gone before I got invited to our first playdate, or even heard back from a mom's group recommending schools or informing me that yes, of course there were other ten-year-olds. We spent our time exploring kid-friendly options, which luckily for us in Medellin, were plentiful. Museums were great, transport was clean and safe, and there were lovely trees lining every street.

My lesson was this: if you have a child and hope to get a sense of the people and families living in a place, then plan ahead and try to locate those families before you arrive. If it's a place you're considering staying long term, or even moving to permanently, then be patient with the discovery process, and don't judge too hastily. It might not be a great, kid-friendly place — or it might have just enough amenities for you and your child to flourish.

Remember that for a child, travel can also be lonely and difficult. Depending on a child's age, it can feel like he or she is being ripped from a comfortable world only to be dragged into discomfort as some parental form of torture. I've experienced all of the above with my son, and then some. So I offer a few tips:

-First of all, make sure you want to travel at all. When your children start throwing tantrums you need to be steady and prepared to support them through this difficult process. You need to know for *yourself* that travel comes with difficulties, so think through it and prepare yourself. Just make sure you always let kids have their emotions.

-Start small. Maybe take a few trips, plan packing and get your kids ready for a variety of adventures. Try different foods ahead of time, and make sure they know that not all places will offer buttered pasta or chicken tenders.

-Travel slow and don't try to fit too much into a short period of time. Travel can be overwhelming and constant change disruptive. Take time to rest and enjoy the small things — like comparing ice cream in every country you visit.

-If siblings are fighting (even more than usual), allow for each to have some time alone, and individual time with a parent. When traveling, kids don't always have the same physical space and quiet time they had at home, so try to create some of that on the road.

-Do some preparation and find some of the most kid-friendly places or activities in a given spot. Then get your kids excited about the places you want to visit. Your son or daughter might not be as excited about visiting the Louvre in Paris as he is to spend hours renting small sail boats to race in the Luxembourg Gardens. He might not be as eager to walk through the streets of a beautiful Mexican city as he might be to discover there is a huge waterpark just outside its walls. Make an effort to find a local zoo, waterpark or playground. For the whole family to be happy it will take compromise on both your parts. Sometimes your child might need to not go out at all. Many parents find that quite time in a hotel room with electronics, art supplies or LEGOs, is exactly what a child needs to rest and get grounded.

Here is one thing I know for sure: if you are a single parent or even a couple traveling with an only child, it will be more difficult for your child than if he or she has a sibling or plans to meet a friend at a given destination. Finding playmates on the road is extremely helpful, and with the growing number of traveling families, it's easier than ever. One summer we announced that we were heading to Europe and asked if any families wanted to meet up. Through that post we ended up traveling with three separate families, one of which we had never met before.

It was no coincidence that Aiden's sadness peaked at three months — what I've come to call the "Three Month Wall". I've since heard repeatedly from families on the road that their children, and this is especially true for only children, also hit a wall at about three months of travel. It's just long enough that the novelty of travel has worn away and the realization begins to set in that they're not heading home to friends in the very near future. Children may act out, begin to talk about wanting to go home, or simply become depressed and withdrawn for a spell. A cranky travel companion is no fun.

Acknowledging and preparing for the difficulties in advance can help get you through them. If you hit this wall, just know that you are not alone, and you may need to be proactive to help your children get to the other side of this impasse. Reach out, ask for advice — so many of us have been there before — and don't give up. There will always be difficult times on the road, as there would be at home, and especially if you have teens. We just have to learn new tools to help us all get through them.

A word here about Third Culture Kids or TCKs. This refers to those of us who grew up in two cultures, traveled frequently, or lived abroad as expat kids for long periods of time. While we may have gained numerous skills in adaptation, flexibility and language, extensive travel also can lead to a sense of rootlessness. TCKs have reported feeling not entirely at home anywhere, whether in their country of "origin" or birth, or where they have spent many years as young people.

Growing up with a French mother and vising family in France each year, I never felt entirely French *or* American. Something always felt off, whether that was my internal gauge or those around me flat out saying I didn't belong. Authors Ruth van Reken and David Pollock studied the phenomenon in their book, *Third Culture Kids: The Experience of Growing Up Among Worlds*. They describe home as an emotional place where you belong, and note that TCKs may not feel they fit into any one culture. Home, writes van Reken is "everywhere and nowhere." The authors call these kids "Cultural Chameleons," adapting where needed but always looking for cues from the culture around them. They may have trouble making plans later in life, or feel grief at always having to say goodbye.

Of course, this book was written at a time before social media connected us all. The positive global citizens your children can become may far outweigh any possible problems. However, it is worth being aware of some of these challenges, and making sure your kids always have a place to express their sadness, even if they aren't sure how to articulate it. As the Worldschooling community grows and also becomes more connected, it is worth making an effort to have your kids meet up with friends they made before in other parts of the world. In this way kids can share what they've been up to and how they experience their new respective locations. As some of the families in this book note, it has been helpful to also create consistent traditions that help children with the transitions of travel and life abroad.

When I asked Aiden if he ever felt some of the unease mentioned in van Reken's book, he shook his head no. "I have friends in this country, and when I go to Mexico I have friends there. It's kind of the best of both worlds."

Chapter 15

Technology on the Road

When we left the US, my kid was an exceptional booka-
holic. We'd go to the library every week and he'd come
home with up to 30 books that he'd pore over night after night. On the road that wasn't so easy. The libraries
we found in Central America had limited — if any —
offerings in English. We bought a Kindle and signed
up to OverDrive, accessing several libraries throughout
the US, but the young adult graphic novels didn't carry
over well into the digital realm.

Which brings us to the question of technology on the
road: how much to have, how to try to avoid it, and
what apps and games are best for educational and entertainment value.

When we started traveling, Aiden was allowed only a
half hour of gaming a night, usually on my computer,
and he didn't have a phone; I thought he was far too
young for such technology. All of that changed, slowly at first, as he wanted to connect with the friends
he missed back home, and then with a bang during

COVID, when his every waking hour seemed to be online for one reason or another.

I had to loosen our rules around tech access. Reading was supplanted by cartoons and educational videos, like the 72 most dangerous animals in Australia — which inspired my son to state in no uncertain terms that we would never, ever be visiting Australia. Educational TV shows started melting into not-so-educational ones. And by the time the worst of COVID had passed, my son was gaming all the time. Initially I resisted. Then I came to appreciate some aspects of his gaming: the story lines, the graphics, the engagement with other players. It was a way to socialize when options were limited, and he did indeed build friendships.

To this day, the friends he met Worldschooling are the ones he still meets online. They play almost daily for hours at a time. They laugh and yell and tell jokes and even talk about travels, as a few of these friends are still on the road.

Tech has changed our lives and we aren't going back. With some boundaries, we can use it as a tool to broaden our horizons and enhance our connections. Those boundaries will vary with each family unit. It should be noted that those of us who now work entirely on-line are never far from our own electronic devices — it is one Faustian bargain with an electronic life that many of us have made to be able to travel full time. On the other hand, the amount of information available in one hand-held device can inform and educate us on almost anything in the world. Like any tool, it has to be used wisely. One of the more ironic photos I took while traveling in Egypt was of Aiden standing at the door of King Tutankhamen's original underground burial site, watching TikTok videos on his phone. He said that after hours spent visiting ancient Egyptian ruins, he needed a break, so I obliged.

In fact, I've let many of my rules around tech fall to the side by now; I've found Aiden makes good decisions and has a group of dear friends from his online life. In the end, I want a positive relationship with my son far more than I want to impose and constantly fight to maintain limitations around his phone use. His safety will always come first, but I have also seen the value he receives from being online. It's a matter for each family to decide.

One skilled parent shared her tech tactics: "During our sabbatical, our kids had to complete their homeschooling work without crying to earn a "LEGO jewel"

HIT THE ROAD!

that could be used to buy screen time. We also had a rule for elementary and middle school and even sometimes years later, that our kids have to read for screen time. When they were younger, they had to read for twice as long as the screen time they earned, so an hour of reading earned them 30 minutes of screen time. As they got older, it became an hour for an hour. We have the Circle [a parental control device] by Disney, which allows us to block certain sites, or set limits, or allow full access on others. Now that they are teens, we sit down together to decide how much time is healthy per each app, or total screen time per day. This is easy to set on iPhones, or there are apps that do this for you. I think it's possible to help kids have a healthy relationship with screens with boundaries and limits that shift as they get older. The ultimate goal being adults with good screen boundaries. We also make sure all our devices go to sleep at a certain time each night, while still allowing audiobooks for going to sleep."

Aiden watching TikTok outside
King Tutankhamun's tomb, Egypt.

Tony and Jade Burke

The Art of Deschooling

"I feel like our kids are actually becoming truer to themselves."

One of the biggest challenges for Canadian couple Tony and Jade, was embracing the process of deschooling — not for their two young children, but for themselves. Deschooling is the process of unlearning and letting go of our traditional school training.

Tony said it was particularly difficult to let go of the idea of traditional schooling since he hadn't gone to college himself, and now in his mid-forties felt like he may have missed some opportunities because of it. He had tried to force homeschooling pages onto his kids, but he saw their walls rise higher and their love of learning start to extinguish.

"We decided to take a step back," said Jade. "We heard about deschooling, that however many years they've been in traditional school is usually the number of months they should have to deschool. Let them be free and then gradually, and naturally, their natural learning desire can come back. And that's what happened. It's coming back now."

Jade said that meeting with other Worldschooling families confirmed to them the value of what they were doing: their decision to eventually unschool wasn't a secondary or lower form of education, but in fact a far more positive experience for them than traditional schooling. It was an epiphany for Tony that he, too, needed to deschool, and it brought relief to know that he wasn't doing it wrong. Once he stopped pushing his kids into something that didn't work, everyone benefited.

In fact, the couple said, it was a film about the outdated education system screened by their school board that became their tipping point towards travel. The documentary, *Most Likely to Succeed*, examined the outdated nature of the North American school system.

"It was about how obsolete the education is, how it was created by ten rich guys over 100 years ago, for factory workers. Those factories have all but disappeared in North America, but the school system set up for them still exists."

The film was a call for schooling to change, and how education should refocus on "soft" skills, such as integrity, communication, professionalism, and critical thinking. Tony and Jade had been thinking about traveling for six months out of the year, and the film was the push they needed. They devised a plan to leave right after their son's birthday in September and come back in time for their daughter's birthday in June, two bookmarks that helped them plan their journey.

Travel hasn't always been easy, but any challenge aside, Jade and Tony noticed something about their children:

"I feel like they're actually becoming truer to themselves," said Jade. "I think they were getting a lot of influence from their classmates about what's cool and what's not cool, and they were masking their true desires. Now we feel like they're being more real and identifying more with what they really like."

As we spoke, Tony pointed to his eight-year-old daughter, who was with a group of teens listening to Disney songs. She had always loved Disney and Princess play, but after a year or two in school "she came back and said, 'I don't like princess stuff. I don't want to wear pink. I like blue now.'" Now she's listening to the Disney Princess Songs again and she's even asking Jade, 'Mommy, can you make my playlist all Disney songs again?' That's a perfect example of her being real again, being herself and true to what she wants."

Tony added another observation: "Whenever we get home, they say they always feel smarter. That's not really measurable, but they just feel more mature and sure of themselves, more confident, more patient, and more tolerant. Being on the road traveling really tests you because it's not easy. It makes them grow."

Tony and Jade are fortunate to share a mobile job running a nursing college and recruiting nurses from overseas. The job takes them to places like India, the Philippines and Brazil, where they attend expos and then extend their travels to have experiences with their kids. They return to Vancouver, BC, for their annual summit, which is one of the few fixed dates around which they organize their travels.

Back in Vancouver, Jade said that the "rat-race" schedule they had before traveling full time was affecting their relationship as a family. Everyone came home grumpy from work and school, and rather than spending time together, they all needed space apart. Now that they're on the road, they're closer and depend on each other more.

"It's actually helped us regroup and get back to where we were prior to the craziness of the business," said Jade. "I think that for our family in particular, it's brought us a lot closer, because you don't have all the craziness of work and school and work and school on repeat. Then suddenly, another year has gone by... Now we're actually able to be together and engage with each other differently and be each other's friends. People often tell you that if you have issues with your relationship, don't think that going traveling is going to fix it. I think that we always had a very strong relationship, which got a little bit rocky with the business. Now that we've gone back on the road, it's gotten back to where it was before, which was strong," Jade said.

Essential Travel Items

Tony: We let the kids have their own stuffed animals.

Jade: Tablets. That's their entertainment, their learning, their YouTube access, their education, and their research.

LEARN

As much as travel is for learning, it also is
a lesson for parents to let go and let our kids explore.
Here, Aiden tries paragliding over the city of Lima Peru,
a birthday request for his 10th birthday.

Chapter 16

Schooling on the Road

"Your Kids will FAIL if you take them out of School!"

If I had a dollar for every time I heard people commenting on the deleterious effects of taking my son out of school, I'd be traveling by private jet from here on out. People are clearly afraid to look beyond a longstanding institutional model of education that is by many accounts clearly outdated. If we learned one thing during the time of COVID it's that kids can and will adapt. Even if they miss classes for a time, with proper encouragement and support, they will catch up — and even excel — once they reenter a learning environment.

Before we talk about the many options for schooling, let's address some of what kids learn by traveling.

Travel can be an amazing and eye-opening education for your children. It can increase their language skills, encourage their independent streak, and help them communicate with and be open to other people and cultures. It challenges their taste buds with new foods, and increases their math skills with every change in currency they encounter. It can grow children's compassion when they see the way so much of the world lives, and it can increase their patience when they realize that things don't always happen as quickly in other countries as they might be used to.

If children are traveling from a country with abundant amenities to one with far fewer, for example, they may see that things aren't so clean or functional as they were back home, or that people are suffering without institutions to care for them. This can give kids a perspective on the relatively opulent middle-class lifestyle they grew up in. Or they might find that some countries have systems that work far better than others. Many countries have exceptional public transportation and healthcare systems. Some honor family connection and are deeply religious. Some might value art, public and otherwise, offer free education, and care for the environment. Many countries offer parental leave and extensive vacation time. (Just a reminder that the United States is one of the only countries *in the world* that does not offer paid parental leave.)

Travel can show your children how to shop for and eat fresh foods from local markets, how to eat less and eat healthier foods in general, and how easy it is to develop sustainable energy sources when there is political will. More than anything it creates resilience and flexibility.

This is all great. But what about schooling?

When I first took my son out of public school, I assumed we would find an online learning program to help guide us throughout our travels. My state did in fact have such a program, but it required Aiden to show up at specific times each day, and I knew our travels couldn't easily accommodate that rigid a schedule. I decided to embrace a period of unschooling, which you've already read a bit about in these pages. Unschooling meant that we would both go through a period of unlearning public school norms, which included stressful Common Core testing requirements and a demeaning emphasis on rules over actual learning that I saw repressing my son's natural learning tendencies and enthusiasm. I wanted my son to completely unplug from his school's curriculum and explore a more "free form" learning model. My extended family members were concerned that he wasn't learning anything at all. It was hard not to absorb their judgment, so we tried homeschooling with an official daily curriculum that covered math, reading and writing. This led to more fights and tears than I could manage.

In Mexico at a family meetup I learned about on Facebook, I met other travelers and learned the term Worldschooling. Worldschooling is learning through travel. These parents would choose locations and historical sites around the world as the basis for lessons in history, math, language and culture. The world was literally their classroom. This fit perfectly for my travels with Aiden, and it became our new model of learning as we continued our travels through Latin America.

With the Worldschooling model in mind, I didn't adhere to any one mode of academic exercise, but I did insist that learning would occur. We learned Spanish and currency conversion, did writing exercises, and scoured online libraries almost nightly for new books. We visited archeological sites and nature reserves, and learned about local customs. Finally, when my son's desire for interaction with other kids was as its height, we settled in a lovely Mexican town, and I registered him in a local English language school. Despite our year without any traditional schooling, my son had no difficulty fitting into his grade.

Most families I meet on the road also try out a range of different learning models. Many left the US specifically because they didn't approve of the educational system in their area, others were horrified by the rash of school shootings across America, and the seeming complete lack of a proper and meaningful response. They were upset with the lack of creativity, arts, or child-specific educational options. And they hated watching a system that, with each passing day, was crushing their children's own creative curiosity.

These parents believe that kids learn when they are engaged and allowed to pursue their own interests. A popular consensus was that US schooling was badly outdated and needed an overhaul. Sure, math and science are vital, as is reading and writing. But many parents felt that the world is changing so fast, technologically and otherwise, and schools aren't considering what our children really need to know in ten or twenty years. And no, this is not a vote for endless computer use and screen time — getting kids outdoors, exploring nature and culture is in fact what Worldschooling does best in my view — but it also is a vote for cultivating creativity, resilience, observation, and people skills.

The most important lesson I came away with was that there are as many ways to learn on the road as there are families traveling. Some parents follow a strict homeschool curriculum; others do all their learning online. Many choose unschooling like we did for a time, and then put their kids in traditional schools in the location they are visiting. And of course each child has a different way of learning, with unique strengths and weaknesses. Some kids love art, others science. Some study better in a group, others alone and in silence. All could benefit from more time outside as exercise and movement helps children concentrate, and improves health and happiness. What good teachers know – and there are so many amazing teachers as well as students strangled by restrictive systems – is that learning should engage and excite. Unfortunately, this doesn't happen in school nearly as much as it should. Many parents have decided to take their kids traveling instead.

Here are some resources to help you explore some of the educational options available. New resources and educational consultants are coming online every day, offering advice, tutoring, and lesson plans.

-Galileo
-Khan Academy
-Udemy

-Adam Ruins Everything
-Science News Magazine
-Vlogbrothers
-Masterclass
-YouTube
-Outschool
-iCivics
-Unschooling/hackschooling
-Omnis Education

There are plenty of online apps that help kids learn:

-iTunes U is an Apple education initiative. Free online courses on a wide range of subjects.
-Coursera – Free, structured online courses on a variety of topics.
-Lynda has video tutorials on a range of subjects, including 3D animation or photography. Subscription based.
-Brightstorm, primarily for teenagers. Provides thousands of videos in a variety of standard school subjects, including calculus and biology. Subscription-based.
-Code Academy provides free coding classes.
-Open Culture has a ton of free educational and cultural media offerings, from speeches, videos, books, lectures and films.

-For younger kids there is FactMonster, CoolMath Games (which my son loved), PBS Kids (Jet Go! And Kratt Brothers were favorites). Thinkrolls Play & Code lets kids solve puzzles, learn critical thinking skills, and build memory and fine motor skills. (3-8). Science 360 and pizza fractions for beginning fraction work.

-For language learning there is Duolingo, Yabla, or Babbel. Music? Try Yousician or Pianu.

There are so many other fun resources that kids can explore and enjoy, such as Now I Know, which sends an email daily with a random bit of information. For example, did you know that Abraham Lincoln created the secret service — on the day he was shot? Now you know.

Education on the road is a big topic for traveling families, and resources for this grow every day. More than academics, however, the goal for many of us who travel is ultimately to help develop kind, compassionate, thoughtful and engaged human beings who are ready to share their talents and skills with a world that desperately needs their help.

Jennifer Sutherland Miller

Rethinking How Kids Learn

"Kids learn so well from their surroundings, so enriching those surroundings is the goal of many traveling parents."

Jennifer started traveling with her husband Tony and their four children in 2008, when the kids ranged in age from five to eleven. Their initial plan was to travel for a year, and they had saved money based on that time frame. Then the market crashed.

"We woke up one morning camped on a sea cliff in Italy. My husband rolled over and said, 'Shit, I think our money is gone.' Most of our money had been in stocks and all of our stock was under water. We found ourselves with hardly any money. We'd sold our house, we'd sold all our stuff, Tony had quit his job with Apple, and here we were with four little kids living in a tent on a cliff in Italy."

Jen said it was, in retrospect, one of the best things to happen to them, forcing them to get intentional about what they wanted out of life and what they wanted to do. Now they had to make some decisions: they could go home and get other jobs or they could find a cheap place to live for a while and figure out the next step. They decided to go to Africa.

That winter the family lived in Tunisia as inexpensively as they could, and started calling in every card they had, trying to recreate their careers. Jen started freelance writing and Tony did database design that grew out of his work at Apple. Three years later, Jen said they were making more money than they'd ever made at their former jobs where they'd worked for twenty years. "Now we were working 20 hours a week while screwing around in the world with our kids," she said.

"We'd found a way to be able to fund our travels, and save money for retirement and for their college, and also really live intentionally with our kids doing the things that we loved to do. That discovery was really game changing for us."

We're getting ahead of ourselves. The couple had always known they wanted to travel with their kids. For Jen, it stemmed from her own childhood, being taken out of school for two separate years to travel through Africa and Central America — what she now calls "the best years of my education, both academically and in terms of life experience and socialization." She knew she wanted something similar for her children.

"I also didn't want to travel with people who were in diapers, because it's just not fun." They waited until their children were school-aged so that the kids would better remember the experience.

The planning took two years, and at the time they didn't have the luxury of online Meet-up groups, Facebook pages and the like. "It was a different world to take off in," she said.

Jen has a degree in education, but she found early on that public schools and traditional classrooms weren't for her. That said, knowing what you don't want and what you *do* want are two wildly different things, she said. She launched into a five-year re-education project, during which she studied philosophy and the history of education, and asked the big question: How did we get here? What is this system about? Are there other ways of thinking about children in life and evolution and the ways we've previously learned?

"What I discovered is that there are very many of those ways. This concept of school happening in a classroom is flawed. School is a delivery device for education, but it is not synonymous with education. Education is not a one-size-fits-all process."

Out of that relearning period the couple developed their own educational philosophy, grounded in multi-level, intergenerational, and real-world learning. The term Worldschooling didn't exist yet — that emerged long after they began traveling — but they did know that the real world would be central in their kids' education. In fact, when her kids were just toddlers, she and her husband sat down and wrote a list of the most important things they wanted their children to learn. The 30-page list included everything from how to read and tie their shoes, to how to can beans and run a chainsaw, to languages. "It sounds ridiculous to me now from the stage of parenthood that I'm in, but at the time it felt important." Above all they wanted their kids to learn independence, freedom, and self-sufficiency.

Jen has since become a resource for families in all things education. Parents come to her for advice, for reassurance that their kids will get into college, and for a curriculum. She suggests that they first decide on their own philosophy of education.

She sees parents who are programmed to think college is the ultimate goal and gateway to financial security, and they come to her terrified that fifteen years down the road their child might not get into the best college.

"As an older mom, now I kind of laugh and say, 'Well, you know, you don't even have him potty trained yet.'"

The reality is that yes, of course they can get into college. Jen knows dozens and dozens of young people who haven't been to traditional school, but have had a wide range of experiences — which turned out to be their biggest selling points.

"We've discovered that good universities are actually looking for that diversity. What they're trying to build are communities of diverse learners and philosophies. That's so hard to do when every single applicant is cookie cutter. In many ways, you do your kids a huge service educationally by getting them outside of the traditional frameworks," she said, adding that the key is measuring their learning in a way that college admissions offices understand and respect.

"All teachers will tell you there's learning happening everywhere. The question is how do we quantify that? As alternative educators, it's our responsibility to be able to translate this really wonderful outside-the-box experience our kids have had into something that the educational establishment can cope with."

To do this, Jen diligently kept track of what her kids were learning and how they were learning. Her daughter's college application included a hefty packet that documented in detail her learning experiences over the years. The process helped each of her children, now grown, get into their first-choice schools, and it didn't necessitate taking standardized tests. Heavy documentation is now something she advises other traveling parents begin to do as well.

Jen has since launched an online learning platform called Omnis Education, "omnis" being the Latin word for "everyone." The idea is that learning does not begin or end at school; it's happening everywhere and always. Primarily for K-12 kids, the program helps people create world-class education outside the classroom. She sees the ed-tech space as a huge growth area — not just for Worldschoolers, but for anyone wanting to enrich their educational experience.

Jen knows there's no one way to do most things. From marriage, career, and parenting, she says if you want to do something different, find the people who are doing that thing, hang out with them and learn from them, and design your own life your way. Same goes for traveling with your kids. "Travel is not better than any other kind of lifestyle, but if it's in your heart to do it, you should definitely do it, because it's a once-in-a-lifetime experience with your kids," she said.

"The thing that I'm learning on the back end is just how fast the whole process of raising kids goes. I can remember thinking when they were four, five and six that Tuesday afternoon felt like it was about six weeks long, and I would probably die before they grew up. Now they're gone. It's amazing how fast that happened.

I'm so grateful that we did the things we did with our kids when we did because it has changed who we are, and our family dynamic. It has changed the relationships we have with each other and with the world, and who they are as professional people. That was a gift from the world."

Essential Travel Items

Carry-on backpacks. I don't like to check luggage or to drag a bunch of stuff around the world. To me, that sucks the joy out of everything. I know that every family travels differently. For us, really good quality travel backpacks were key.

We always invested in the best quality clothing, shoes and gear that we possibly could, because those kinds of points of failure tend to damage your calm when you're on the road.

"You can buy anything you need in the world, anywhere that there are people. Maybe not everything you want, but everything you need. Just take the people who are meaningful with you and everything else works itself out."

Jen suggests that as your child is growing and learning, to keep a detailed journal or Google file, and every week make notes:

What did we learn this week?

Where did we go?

What did we do, and which museum was coolest?

What fabulous idea did my child have this week?

"If you just take a few minutes to do this, week, by week, it's shocking how fast the learning adds up. It becomes easy on the back end to quantify what you've done."

Chapter 17

Single Parent or Solo Travel

I mentioned the importance of preparation and trusting your gut when traveling. This is particularly important when you are a single parent or simply traveling alone.

Let's begin with a reality check: traveling as a single parent is a lot of work. You do everything. There is no one else to share the costs, plan the trip, make the reservations, make sure everyone is safe, fed, sheltered in strange lands, cared for if sick, etc. It's all you, babe. Depending on the age of your child or children, it can also be quite lonely. You might not be able to share the stories or enjoy the things that you would with another adult. If your child is older, he or she may just want to be home with friends (or complain endlessly whether or not it's true). With multiple children there's a chance one can watch the others while you grocery shop, shower, or go to the bank, but you're still the full-time travel agent and financier of this adventure.

If this sounds familiar, I'd suggest going back to your *why* of traveling to help get you through the tough parts.

A brief reminder of some benefits:

-To expose your children to different cultures, people, and experiences.

-To spend time with your child that might not be possible in the 9-to-5 schedule of your home life.

-To save money, because as we know, it can be more affordable to travel full time than to be in one place in a high-priced location and home.

Even with the easiest of children, travel can be a challenge. Now imagine a child with sensory difficulties trying to make it through the security line at an airport. One mom wrote me that the only way her son would go through the security check was on his hands and knees barking like a dog. They barely made their flights.

Below are some of the challenges most commonly expressed by single parents when traveling, and some hacks to help make it easier.

Feeling lonely—this goes for you or your child

Connect with listservs in various countries. Call home. Skype and Zoom. Let your child see and hear his or her friends. Sometimes group video game playing is a savior. Look for parenting groups or single mom groups in the place you are visiting. Even on a general list-serv or Facebook group, asking about family meet-ups can provide connections.

There are differing opinions on the value of returning home for a while, particularly if your teens (and it's often the teens who most crave social interactions) claim they are miserable. Two bits of advice: allow enough time to really get into travel mode. Teens may say they are miserable because their bodies are changing, their hormones are raging. They are having perfectly normal ups and downs and it's very easy to blame any emotional or social difficulty on travel — or on you. In this case it's good to check in with friends back home because often you'll hear the same difficulties are happening at home as on the road.

However, if your teen continues to be miserable after eight months or a year traveling, consider whether it might be best for you all — or simply the teen — to return home, either for a short time, or permanently. Just be prepared in the event he or she wants to stay put once you're ready to get back on the road. I found that once I reminded my son that school would start by the end of the month, and his friends were too busy buying their back-to-school supplies to play with him, he was eager for us to leave again. Your child might love the familiarity and comfort of home, but parents who travel with their kids have said repeatedly that children know intuitively that their experiences are special, even if they don't understand how. They eventually see that they are changing in ways that are different from their friends back home.

General Safety Tips

Teach your children whom to call if there is an emergency, what to do if you get lost and where to meet if you should get separated. This includes what to do if one child fails to get on or off the bus or metro at the right stop. Make sure they have the name, address, and phone of the place you're staying, and learn how and when to call a "911" version in the country you're visiting. In India, for example, they launched 112 as an emergency help line in 16 states.

I use an app called Life360 that tracks Aiden's whereabouts via his phone. It only works when he has WiFi and juice in the phone's battery, but it gives me comfort when he is out with friends.

Have a codeword that only you and your child or children know, in case a stranger tries to pick up your child and says he or she is there by your request. Make sure your child has information on him to tell officials where he is staying in the event he gets lost. Many put this info in a child's shoe or a zip pocket. Some families take daily photos of their child or children to better recall their clothing.

Many families travel with a carbon monoxide detector, to warn people in the event of dangerously high levels of carbon monoxide (often from leaking gas appliances and heating systems), particularly near sleeping areas.

If you go out on your own, walk with purpose and stand upright. Don't wear valuables or revealing clothing in conservative countries. Err on the side of being conservative, particularly in Muslim countries. This isn't blaming the victim, but simply being respectful and staying safe. In many countries, wearing a headscarf is not only respectful, but will ward off some unwanted glances. In several countries I've worn a gold band on my hand even though I'm not married.

It is unlikely that something will happen, but it is always good to be prepared, whether you're traveling abroad or at home.

What many parents learn while traveling is that people will help you. Perfect strangers will lend a hand in the most amazing and unexpected ways. When I last drove out of Mexico I saw strangers suddenly pull over and jump out of their cars to help push a broken down vehicle towards a nearby gas station. This car wasn't in the way; it was simply a decent thing to do to help this one motorist get the help he needed. Another time a friend and I pulled a stranded car off a jungle road, even though we were late for an appointment. My friend's truck had towing equipment and we knew that had it been us stranded, a Mexican would have done the same.

That said, you should always have your eyes open and don't accept invitations that seem sketchy. Trust your gut but also stay open to those who are willing to help in any emergency.

Documents

The documents suggested in Chapter 10 are particularly important when traveling solo.

Again, make sure you have a copy of your child's birth certificate and/or a letter from the other parent, hopefully allowing longer or more frequent trips.

While it's the last thing on many people's minds — we are still feeling immortal, after all — accidents happen and when you're a single parent, you must be responsible enough to ensure your papers are in order. In my case, there is no close family member to take over, so I designated guardianship to dear friends back home in the event that anything were to happen to me. I also own a car and a house, so I always have an updated Last Will and Testament.

Another essential document, particularly if you are a homeowner or have other assets, is Power of Attorney in the event you are incapacitated. This (hopefully very trusted) person can make legal decisions regarding your assets and care for your child or children.

Ways to connect

As the traveling community grows, there are more and more ways to connect, and single parents and larger families are finding ways to travel together or meet up along the way. This not only provides greatly-needed social connections for kids, but also opportunities for adults to share their triumphs and challenges. Some of the most common ways to connect include Facebook groups like Women Who

Travel, Single Moms Abroad, Single Moms in Mexico, Worldschoolers, etc.

Increasingly, folks are launching organized family travel groups like Karen King's WorldSchooling Central or Lainie Liberti's Project Worldschooling groups for teens and families. There are organized meetups, where families gather for up to a month and share skills and stories so all may benefit. Increasingly, there are paid family gathering centers, like Anahata Worldschooling Community in the Yucatán, Mexico, which has 1-3 month "sessions" where families live on site.

Sex and dating

One day, some traveling friends and I were sharing stories of sex and love. I had told them some of the more entertaining come-ons I'd experienced as a single woman traveling in Mexico, and how I was reluctant to date until I could get a better sense of local traditions. My friend, who was married and had no dating stories to tell, shared his tale of how travel improved his sex life. He and his wife had recently left the Mormon Church, where he'd grown up believing sex was shameful and only for procreation, not for enjoyment. Travel challenged that. "Sex only got better once I left the church.

We simply didn't know that we were allowed to enjoy it this much." His story stayed with me, and reminds me once again that sometimes we have to change our environment to change our mind.

I'll admit I'm more cautious now that I'm a single mom, and also because in each new place there can be social norms and signals that aren't always easy to understand. For example, I got asked out on many dates — only to find out the person was married. In Mexico a man might have a male lover on the side. I also know that as a white, American woman, I represent wealth, however financially challenged I may feel in my own country, the truth is that some people see foreigners, and Americans in particular, as a potential ticket out of the lives they are living. Many also see us as sexually more accessible and with fewer sexual hang-ups. I'm not here to moralize on anyone's sexual desires, but simply to lay bare the assumptions sometimes made about travelers.

If dating does not happen organically, you can try common dating apps, which are as prevalent in other countries as they are in the US: Tinder, Bumble, Hinge, OK Cupid, Craigslist, etc., as well as gay and lesbian sites.

If you do go out on a date, find a trustworthy babysitter recommended by other expats in the area. This may even be the child of another expat or the expat him or herself. In lower-cost areas, it's easy to find a full-time nanny for days or weeks if need be. Parents with young kids have recommended starting with local Facebook groups. Always connect with families where you are and make sure to get references. Care.com and sittercity.com work in the US; the International Nanny Association (nanny.org) or momji.fr, which also lists international nanny and babysitter services, are places to start for international care.

Single parent challenges are very real, whether at home or abroad. But so often living abroad can allow single parents a greater ability to support their children more comfortably than they could at home. Lower costs of living can be a game changer for parents who might otherwise be working three jobs just to afford childcare. Mothers I met said they could finally breathe more easily, and could actually spend time with their children without the constant chasing of the almighty dollar. Now they could afford childcare, household help, and transportation.

I'll end this chapter as I end many of my travel days: reminding myself of the benefits of single parent travel:

-People help more readily and are open to you when you're a solo parent, whether mother, father or guardian.

-It's easier to find accommodations. Simply being a smaller unit or female will help if you're looking to make personal connections or do family stays.

-You don't have to ask permission from another parent. I know some single parents don't have this luxury, but many of us do. A side note: if you know from the beginning that the father of your baby won't be around for any of your child's life and you're unsure about whether to put the father's name on the birth certificate, dear Lord please don't! Just don't. This can and will save you from so much potential hassle in the long run.

-As anyone knows, the more people making decisions, the slower it goes. As a single parent traveling, you get to make all the decisions yourself, and therefore travel more swiftly. Caveat: Include your children in the decision-making process when they are old enough. Let your kids decide where they want to visit based on books they've read or history they want to learn. Even young children can help decide if they want to go to a park or eat an ice cream instead. The point is to empower them early.

-Finally, remember that you've created an opportunity to experience the world with these love(s) of your life. Make it Fun. Laugh as much as possible. Eat ice cream. Take downtime. Do what you want to do, not what you "should" do. And remember that the time you actually have with your child or children will be gone in a flash.

Caroline

The Logistical Rubik's Cube

"One thing that hasn't changed in eight years is the amount of decision-making there is."

I thought I was skilled at traveling with a child. Then I met Caroline.

Caroline is a full-time Worldschooler whose online job is to help other homeschooling families, so educational requirements are familiar for her.

When I met Caroline, she was just shy of 40, traveling with her three children, all under age ten. A Canadian citizen, she told me she began world traveling during a long delay in processing her children's passports. It's what she called an opportunity.

They began by driving across Canada, then once the passports arrived they shipped their caravan (motorhome) to the Netherlands and continued on through Europe. That was eight years ago, and they have yet to stop.

"One thing that hasn't changed in eight years is the amount of decision-making there is. I call it the logistical Rubik's cube," Caroline said. "One of the challenges is that there are so many options. When the world is limitless, it makes it difficult to pin down where we're going to go next, what we're going to do next, and how we can do everything while living within or below our means."

What has proven most helpful to Caroline is finding a place to anchor, like Mexico for a Worldschooling conference, or her son's theater camp in London. Then they make their other travel plans around that.

"That's how we make sure that we do things that everybody wants to do."

All three children continue to embrace the adventure of travel wholeheartedly, though a growing challenge is continually having to say goodbye to people. "We often talk about the fact that if we don't say goodbye, then we won't have the next experience."

Caroline is fortunate that her children not only enjoy traveling, but they get along well, and enjoy being together. They've also become resilient and flexible travelers. An eight-hour car ride for them is just another day, she said.

"We always say, 'this is the plan, but plans can change,' so they take things in stride. That's really helpful for them and for me."

It also helps that Caroline's daily work feeds into and informs her own life. She assesses her own children's learning as she does that of her clients, making sure they establish themselves in a new place with classes and new learning experiences. Routine is important wherever they may be, yet she's happy to let go of things that weren't working well or that her kids didn't enjoy.

One lesson they've learned is that people make the place. "Places where we've made good friends are always more interesting to go back to than places that had really exciting amenities or nice museums."

Caroline's advice to those starting out is to start small and do nothing overwhelming. "Start with small trips or weekend trips, and get a bigger sense of the world before you leave. Maybe where you live there's a Chinatown and when you go there it sparks your kids' interest."

Try to figure out what they're interested in before planning a long, expensive trip that they might resist from start to finish. Having their buy-in is important, she said, though it isn't always easy to get, and can shift. However, it can make for far easier traveling.

Like many travelers, Caroline saves money when she's on the road; living stationary in Canada is often far costlier. And she has found creative ways to experience things that might otherwise be outrageously expensive. Take Disney World, which can cost a family of four upwards of $400 a day.

"My kids were really excited about the idea of going to Disney World. Anytime you look into a Disney World vacation, the number of dollar signs just keep popping up. It didn't seem to make sense to me to spend so much money on what becomes a high stakes experience, where if somebody gets sick or something comes up it's a big expenditure."

Instead, she planned a visit to Florida for three months, living at a campsite just outside the Disney World park.

"I took advantage of every kind of discount I possibility could. I bought a yearly Disney World pass for each one of our family, and only went into the actual park maybe one or two hours a day at most. We spent the rest of our time at the campsite. The kids loved it because there were other families on vacation there."

The kids had full use of the pool and all the resort amenities. Caroline could get work done while the kids participated in activities like dance parties or swimming alongside a Disney counselor.

"We could experience Disney World in a way that other people would never experience it. We could go for only an hour, and just stand and have a conversation with somebody." They often went in with other families they met at the campsite, and they never felt rushed like those who only had one day to see everything. By the time they left, they were fully satisfied with every aspect of their experience. Importantly, the entire stay fell within their monthly budget.

The area where Caroline makes no compromise is in their access to WiFi. It's essential for her work, not to mention what she jokingly refers to as her third job, which is doing all the logistical planning of their travels.

"Having my computer and access to the internet is definitely something that I spend a lot of time on, figuring out how to make sure we have it, and that we're always connected."

Caroline has traveled for long enough that she has seasoned advice for those starting out.

"We have these dreams and cultural experiences we want our families to have, and often we ended up trying to do so much. For us it has worked a lot better to find something small that gives us a sense of where we are, but that we experience with some depth. It could just be eating in the same place every day and getting to know the restaurant owners, and becoming more comfortable with a food that they weren't comfortable with before. That can happen when you focus on one small bit instead of hoping to do everything. We leave a lot of places saying, 'next time we can do this.' That way, we don't have this feeling that we didn't see that place or that site. We went to Paris, and we didn't go to the Eiffel Tower. We didn't leave with this feeling of, 'Oh, we didn't do it all'. We can always say, 'next time, next time we can do that.'"

Essential Travel Items

Access to WiFi.

Chapter 18

Wellness and
Health Care on the Road

One of my most frightening traveling experiences occurred while I was traveling in Cambodia, when Aiden was only three years old. I was spending three months in the country traveling to towns and villages and interviewing survivors of the Khmer Rouge for my master's thesis on conflict management and storytelling. Luckily, Aiden was too young to understand the stories and just innocent enough to adore the warmth of the people — and the relative affordability of big and fast toy trucks. We purchased a go-cart that he would ride each evening on a path bordering the Mekong River. He would peddle for hours, encouraging other kids to hitch rides and run after him, before giving in to exhaustion and letting me take him home.

It could have been the pollution, the heat, or a combination of several factors. Aiden had been suffering from some kind of respiratory infection, which wasn't terrible but didn't seem to improve despite repeated treatment. A doctor at the hospital in Phnom Penh told me he'd be fine, but if for some reason he started to have trouble breathing I should take him immediately to a hospital. The next day, as we drove to a small jungle town next to the Thai border, I noted in my mind a giant hospital building. Just in case. We ate a nice dinner and went to bed in our simple hotel room.

In the middle of the night I awoke to Aiden's labored breathing. It sounded like a train rumbling over a track made of boulders. I snapped to attention and immediately woke my colleague, who then woke our driver. If the Phnom Penh doctor was right, I needed to get my son medical care — and fast. I gave him a dose of Benadryl and we loaded into the car and raced to the hospital, his little body still laboring to breathe. We got to the front of the towering building, and I jumped out of the car. In the darkness, and carrying my now limp boy in my arms, I made my way to the front entrance. It was locked. And chained shut. With nothing inside! The entire building was empty.

The building I later learned was a shell, donated to the region by a generous NGO. Yet they hadn't given enough money for the equipment to fill the hospital, or for the staff to staff the hospital, or for the electricity to even light the damn place. My heart sank and I started to cry. Why was I even *in* Cambodia? Would my son be OK? Would we all die in this remote country? Had I been so selfish as to jeopardize my son's life because I was so intent on getting a Master's degree?

We did find a doctor that night, who lived in a nearby house. His annoyed housekeeper reluctantly let us in, no doubt moved by the boy in my arms. We waited an hour for the doctor to join us. When he finally examined Aiden he said the boy was in fine shape. No need for alarm. He was asleep and breathing as normally as could be expected given his respiratory infection. Go home, he told us. We left the next day back to Phnom Penh, cutting our trip short by three days.

Aiden eventually recovered, but only after I "kidnapped" him out of the Cambodian hospital against doctor's orders and flew him to Thailand for better care.

My self-flagellation for my lack of preparation in that moment went on for years, and ultimately changed the way I traveled. In fact, we stopped traveling for several years, at least until I sensed my son had a stronger immune system. I vowed that any place I visited from there onward would have an established medical system with competent doctors. When I begin to research a potential destination, some of my first questions now are about doctors and hospitals. I want to know in advance where the health facilities are and whom to contact in an emergency. I also chose to fully vaccinate my son, though not in the traditional way prescribed by Western pediatricians. Instead, I spread the vaccines out over time in a way that felt more aligned with my beliefs and comfort level.

It is, of course, very stressful to have a hurt or sick child while traveling — or to be sick yourself, especially if you're far from resources and comforts, and familiar or even accessible transportation. If one or more of you get sick, reach out and find a friend to walk you through, even if only online. One time I used Skype to show my doctor friend back in the US a red rash spreading across my son's belly — which turned out to be scarlet fever!

Years later we happily traveled again to poorer countries with substandard medical systems. By then, I felt confident about my son's health and more able to navigate an online and real-time support. I've since had major surgery in foreign countries, and the most valuable asset I had, besides medical insurance, was a group of expat friends who rallied around me and supported my entire medical journey. That was priceless indeed.

My personal medical kit includes:

Colloidal silver, Band-Aids, tweezers, Neosporin, antibiotics, Benadryl, children's Tylenol, aspirin, lots of Vitamin C, a good thermometer, gauze and bandages. Rescue Remedy drops or candies and a good multivitamin and immune booster. For airplanes: Calms Forté, a homeopathic sleep aid; eyedrops; Dramamine, if one is prone to motion sickness; Tums for minor stomach upset; liquid Band-Aids, anti-flu packets such as Theraflu; and Oscillococcinum, a homeopathic remedy for flu, to be taken immediately upon the first symptom.

This is my own personal list; you should consult with your physician to create a medical kit that works for you and your family.

Paying for my Mexican surgery in cash.

Pati and Andrew Goodell

Choosing Opportunity
When It Presents Itself

"It just didn't add up for us to live in the United States."

Pati and Andrew contemplated travel for years, and knew well the fragility of life: Andrew's father had died suddenly at 43. The Portland, Oregon family had spent five years downsizing and simplifying their lives, unknowingly preparing for a life they were about to start.

"Along the way, we confirmed our belief that bigger is not necessarily better and that possessions aren't what bring true and lasting happiness. For us, sharing new experiences and time together are what is most fulfilling."

When Pati lost her job at a consulting company, they saw it as an opening to do what they'd contemplated for years: traveling with their son Ethan. The logical and safe thing to do in this situation would have been to go out and get another job, she said, which she was confident could be done.

"Instead, we decided to see this as an opportunity for an even more dramatic change. This was a blessing in disguise and an unexpectedly welcome catalyst."

They traveled throughout Southeast Asia, Europe and then to Central America. At first, they lived off the savings from the sale of their home. Then Pati got a full-time job through past contacts with a small copywriting and content strategy agency. In Northern Mexico, where the family of three ultimately landed, they were able to live comfortably off only one salary.

"Traveling is not as expensive or as logistically challenging as you might think," she said. "Depending on your approach, it's often cheaper than living in the US. For us, we simply needed to decide what our priority was — a house filled with stuff, comfort and familiarity... or travel."

Will they go back? Well, their story is complicated. Their son has a chronic condition that requires a monthly injection. In the US the cost before they left was $1000 a month — with insurance — and that amount would increase as their son grew and required a greater dose. Pati guessed that amount would have increased to nearly $3000 a month since they left the US, plus the cost of their insurance premium, which in 2014 was $800 a month. In Mexico, unlike the United States (and thanks to Obamacare), pre-existing conditions can be excluded from any policy. Still, Pati pays about a third what she would in the US out of pocket, plus roughly $3000 a year for the whole family to be insured.

"It just didn't add up for us to live in the United States."

Essential Travel Items

An unlocked phone.

Chapter 19

Travel Insurance

A word — or five — about insurance: Make Sure You Have It.

I have met many traveling families who over time allowed their health insurance to lapse because, as they described it, "Medical costs are low enough we can pay for services out of pocket." In general, this is true. You will be amazed at the relatively low costs of basic procedures that in the US might wipe out a year's savings. However, small procedures are not the purpose of health insurance. In the US, we pay exorbitant amounts for health insurance so we don't go bankrupt should we get very sick or injured. The same is true abroad.

You will almost certainly suffer some kind of ailment while on the road. The most common problems include minor or not-so-minor stomach upsets from eating new foods, drinking local water, or not washing your hands. Digestive problems doesn't indicate that the location is unclean, but rather that your body needs time to adjust; most of these ailments will go away within a few days as your intestinal flora and fauna get used to your new environment. Another common problem is altitude sickness, for example if you're going from sea level to high-altitude locations like San Miguel de Allende in Mexico or Machu Picchu in Peru. Symptoms of altitude sickness like headaches or extreme fatigue can usually be addressed by drinking lots of water and resting for a few days upon arrival.

While they are unlikely, you should be prepared for more serious emergencies, like a car accident, a serious fall, or the need to repatriate remains if the worst should happen. Accidents happen anywhere and everywhere, and it's important that you and your family have insurance.

What Kind of Insurance Should I Get?

There are two basic types of health insurance available to travelers: international health insurance and travel insurance. Generally speaking, international health insurance is for people living overseas for longer periods, while travel insurance covers emergencies during shorter stays. Travel insurance also covers lost luggage, cancelled flights, and a short-term emergency while you get yourself home for better care. International health insurance will cover routine checkups, hospital stays, and coverage for preexisting or chronic conditions.

In fact, many countries, like Cuba and Egypt, now require visitors to have a travel insurance.

I advise you do your own research, as the quality or reputation of an insurance company can change, but here are few companies popular among travelers:

SevenCorners.com
Allianze.com
TravelInsurance.com
RoamRight.com
WorldNomads.com
TrawickInternational.com

An American friend visiting India reminded me of the benefits of health insurance. After suffering a heart attack, he got first-rate emergency surgery, plus a flight home accompanied by a nurse's aide, all for a fraction of what he would have paid in the US. I've had to cancel flights for medical reasons and received a full refund — though not without a significant amount of bureaucratic paperwork.

Medical Tourism

Which brings us to the topic of medical tourism, which I'll touch on briefly.

A statistic that has always stayed in my mind is that the majority of Americans who file for bankruptcy do so because of medical bills. Of those, the majority had medical insurance. Take my friend Duke, who was diagnosed with Hepatitis C after being offered a "free" tattoo by a popular jungle shaman years ago in Ecuador. Who could refuse that? Hep C is transmitted by blood-to-blood contact, often by sharing needles or using unsanitized tattoo equipment. Sometimes Hepatitis C is asymptomatic, but can kill you in short order if it's not. And it can lie dormant for years.

By the time he was diagnosed many years later, a drug cocktail had been developed in the United States. The price tag: $95,000, which his insurance refused to cover. A fearless world traveler, Duke knew this treatment had to be available elsewhere. He eventually flew to India for treatment, including a full liver scan to be sure there was no lasting damage. The cost? $6,000. That's right, a savings of almost $90,000! According to my friend, the treatment and care were as professional as he'd experienced anywhere.

Others may travel thousands of miles for affordable cosmetic procedures, such as facelifts, breast implants and the like. A friend flew to Thailand for extensive dental surgery; another flew to the Philippines to have his hip replaced. I continue to consult my dermatologist and get dental check-ups whenever I visit Mexico.

Some of the fastest-expanding areas for medical tourism include Colombia; Thailand; Ecuador, and the Philippines. Thailand is among the best known, and has extensive English-speaking facilities. Even India is becoming a big player in the health tourism game.

Make sure you conduct extensive research on any country or health facility before considering going overseas for a procedure.

Aiden has rarely met an animal he didn't like. He assured
me these monkeys at the Monkey Forest in Bali weren't
going to hurt him because he stayed so calm. I reminded
him that rabies often comes from monkey bites.

Aldis Barketis

The 411 on Expat and Traveler Insurance

"We have a saying: don't be that GoFundMe campaign person."

Based in San Miguel de Allende, Mexico, Aldis has been running an expat insurance agency for years, with offices in Mexico and Thailand. He mainly serves clients from the US and Canada, but he shares insurance advice for short- and long-term travelers the world over. We're going to go into the weeds here because health insurance is a big, hairy topic for those wanting to live abroad.

Aldis' advice is simply this: regardless the insurance company you choose, buy insurance if you plan to travel. Period. He's seen too many GoFundMe cases by families who assumed the worst wouldn't happen to them. You can go bankrupt abroad just as you can in the United States. In some countries, like Mexico, if you get in a car accident and need surgery, they are not required to treat you unless there is proof that they will be paid, usually in cash. Unless you have easy access to $10, $20 or even $100,000 dollars, your best bet is to buy health insurance.

To determine the best policy, Aldis begins by asking a question: What coverage do you have in your home country, and will that follow you? Many Americans who are not yet retired may have access to their company health plans, or a Cobra plan (continuation of coverage) they can pay into after leaving their work. If they have a plan through the Affordable Care Act (Obamacare), their policies likely will cover them for emergencies abroad. However, I strongly recommend calling your current insurance provider to see what their coverage provides before you travel.

People on Medicare will likely need supplemental plans to cover themselves abroad, though that coverage is meant for shorter trips up to 60 days. This is not sufficient for those wanting to live abroad.

"Medicare supplements are really built to take care of somebody going on a cruise or going to Europe for a month, and they work on a reimbursement basis,"

Aldis said. If an insurance company suspects you've been traveling much longer, they could ask to see your passport to make sure an accident happened within the time frame of the supplement."

For Canadians it's more complicated, with provincial care covering citizens who are out of the country for less than six months. Any more than that and you lose your coverage. "Even if you're 80 years old, you lose your provincial plans," Aldis said.

If you're planning to live abroad, there are two ways to protect yourself. One is a short-term travel policy; you're basically renting additional insurance for the time of your trip. The process is simple and doesn't require you to provide health information. Those policies are meant for unexpected accidents and illness — a broken leg, a scooter accident. The companies that provide these policies don't know anything about you. Such plans are risky if anything should actually go wrong during a long-term stay.

"It's very important, at the bare minimum, to get a travel policy, because things can get really expensive, really quick abroad," Aldis said. Just know that if you go to renew your travel policy and have suffered a health issue in the interim, there may be exclusions.

The second way to cover yourself is to purchase a major international medical policy, which requires you to answer a long list of medical and health questions. Depending on how you respond, the company may not cover you, or may exclude some of your health issues, like cancer or diabetes treatment. Absolutely consult an insurance company or agent, particularly if you have any health issue.

If you choose to go with an international policy, there are some considerations:

Where do you want coverage? If your travel is limited to Latin America, then buy a policy that provides coverage in Latin America. Or you can buy a worldwide policy for broader world travel.

Another option is a major medical policy that covers you worldwide, including the US. The companies that offer these policies require that you be outside of the US for more than six out of 12 months.

This may feel overwhelming, but take my advice and study your options, as having health insurance is essential.

"It drives me nuts when people say 'I'm moving to Mexico, care is cheap, I'm just going to self-insure.' Well, do a Google search for GoFundMe campaigns and you'll find so many sad stories," Aldis said. 'Henry is in intensive care, and he needs back surgery and we're trying to raise $35,000 for him.' Or, 'this couple was in Cancun and the hospital won't release them unless the $70,000 bill is paid.'"

"We have a saying: don't be that GoFundMe campaign person. If you self-insure yourself, just make sure you have a liquid $10, $20 or $30,000 ready to go for any disaster. Alternatively, purchase an insurance policy."

If you're an American and you're considering moving abroad, Aldis suggests you get important check-ups and screenings, which are usually included in health coverage, such as a colonoscopy, mammogram, and blood work.

He also suggests getting all of your medical records. If you have some sort of a health condition — let's say you're on a cholesterol and blood pressure medication — and you apply for health insurance, the underwriter can simply do a cardiac exclusion, he said. Remember, unlike Obamacare in the US, pre-existing conditions are not necessarily covered in other countries.

Or if you had cancer seven years ago, get those medical records. "The odds are that if you've had breast cancer seven years ago, you are in the same risk category as somebody who has not had cancer. But the underwriter is going to say, 'I want to know what happened seven years ago. Do you have a record of that?' 'Yes, I do. Here it is.'"

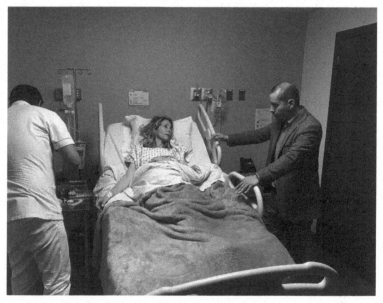

Friends suggested I return to the US for surgery but
I declined. In the end, the cost of my care — albeit
with some complications — was a fraction of
comparable surgeries I read about in the US.

MONEY

When we began our long-term travel,
we lived off of rental income. Then I found I
could do the same amount of writing and audio editing
while traveling. Here we are in our first month of travel
at the pyramids outside Mexico City, Mexico.

Chapter 20

Financing Your
Travel/Jobs on the Road

One of the most common questions for long-term travelers is how to finance their journeys. Like so much in this book, the answers are as different and creative as the people traveling. A common assumption is that the majority of travelers are independently wealthy or "trust funders." Yes, some are. However, many travelers I've encountered are not — but they have a level of creativity and resourcefulness that any fortune 500 CEO might envy. They have saved, inherited, worked on the road, or worked during restaurants' high season in order to travel during the off season. They are "stay at home" parents or work their way through each country bartending or crafting as they go. One mom I met sells used underwear. Most of us work remotely.

As a freelance journalist, I have always been scrappy and resourceful and have found ways to live well on a modest annual income. In a sense, I was lucky in that I never had a large salary to give up.

Interestingly, I learned more about money and financial responsibility while traveling than I ever had at home. With my new-found extra time, I began learning about savings and investing. I learned about retirement funds for me and college funds for my son. I joined a group discussing real estate investing, side hustles, and how much a person might need to retire early (roughly 25 times your annual expenses). I learned a bit about day trading, and above all how important, wonderful, and possible it is to become financially independent.

Some of the biggest lessons I learned were about bad debt versus good debt (pay off those credit cards! versus a mortgage which builds equity), how to build wealth through investing and real estate, and how to live with less.

How do I do it? I'm fortunate to own a house in the US that I can rent out, and I don't have any student debt. These two things alone put me financially ahead of millions of Americans. At the same time, I am a single mother who worked full time and struggled to support her family. The very reason I left for a life of travel was to be able to slow down and save money while deciding on my next step.

This concept is called Geoarbitrage, and it means taking advantage of the different costs of living in various locations. In other words, moving to a place with a lower cost of living to save money or to have a better lifestyle. You've already heard many of these stories in this book.

If you are a remote worker who earns money in US dollars, and depending on the exchange rate of various currencies, those dollars can buy much more in some countries than others. I personally don't travel in luxury (my son, however, has other ideas, and thinks room service should be the baseline for choosing a hotel) nor do I spend a lot of time in countries with a high cost of living. Each person has a different budget, and you must plan accordingly. Sites like expatistan.com or numbeo.com offer suggestions, including country comparisons and cost of living estimates. Nomadlist.com, a paid site, can help you compare the cost of living of various cities, including average rents and food prices. The US consistently is listed as having the highest costs.

It's important to note that you may not earn the same amount on the road as you did in your full-time job, unless you are keeping your full-time job and taking it with you. Remote work options may not pay you as much, at least at the outset, but you won't need as much.

Most countries will not allow you to get a job without a work permit, so for travelers, remote work is often the only option. As its popularity grows, countries are seeing the benefits that remote workers bring, as money earned elsewhere is spent locally, often supporting struggling economies. In fact, the emergence of COVID inspired many countries to offer extended visas and great WiFi specifically to entice digital nomads (referring to travelers who work online). These visas are now available for Barbados, Costa Rica, Croatia, Malta, Norway, Spain, Portugal and Dubai among others. To access these visas you often are required to show a minimum monthly income. Be aware of a country's tax policies and follow all laws.

Where Money is Concerned, Mindset is a Must

If you're planning to travel and you're concerned about how to afford it, know this: mindset and attitude matter more than anything else. You must have the desire. This is perhaps the most important piece of information in this book. I believe, and hundreds of families I've met on the road would agree, that if you really, truly want to travel, you will find a way. Mindset won't pay for a plane ticket, but it just might help you see outside the box with more resourcefulness and creativity. If you wish you could afford to travel, then a good first step is to be inspired by the many ways people have made travel happen. Travelers are rich and they are poor. They are American and international. Their skin is of every shade. They all wanted to travel, and they all found a way. For many, the first step was financial education.

Financial Education

There are innumerable books, blogs and amazing podcasts about finances. Here are a few that have helped change my money mindset and encouraged me to create a life that balances retirement savings and a life of travel:

The 4-Hour Work Week

One of my biggest inspirations before I left the US for years of travel was the book *The 4-Hour Work Week* by Tim Ferriss. It changed the way I think about work and inspired me to take a leap of faith and rethink my life path. I wasn't yet ready to quit my job, but it opened my mind to other work possibilities. It also taught me to be more creative. Tim has since started a podcast in which he conducts deep dive interviews with interesting people. He also has written more books, including *Tools of Titans*, a bestseller in which he interviews top performers and leaders about their habits, tools and philosophies.

Denise Duffield-Thomas is a money mindset coach and author of numerous books, including *Get Rich Lucky Bitch* and *Chillpreneur*. Her work around Money Archetypes opened my eyes to many of the ways I was sabotaging my own work.

Jen Sincero – As a self-described badass mom, I was thrilled when someone gifted me this book. Little did I know how powerful the message, not only about owning one's life, but on making money. *You Are a Badass; How to Stop Doubting Your Greatness and Start Living an Awesome Life*, *You Are A Badass at Making Money*. #Badassery

Die With Zero: Getting all you can from your Money and Your Life by Bill Perkins. The premise of this book is that people should be maximizing their life enjoyment and not just wealth accumulation.

The hedge fund manager does suggest funding a basic retirement before maximizing life enjoyment, which might defeat his premise in the mind of some travelers. He correctly writes that by waiting until retirement, one may not have the physical ability or even desire to take on some bucket list adventures.

Mr. Money Mustache (the pseudonym for Canadian Peter Adeney) is a blog all about saving that has a cult-like following. Mrmoneymustache.com

Making sense of Cents is a fantastic newsletter and blog by Michelle Schroeder-Gardner with great savings and side hustle tips. She also offers courses for starting a blog or affiliate marketing, among others. Makingsenseofcents.com

Bigger Pockets is a website started by Brandon Turner about real estate, including investing essentials, a wide variety of podcasts and links to classes and documents. While Brandon gets granular about real estate, the ultimate goal is to create time and financial independence. Biggerpockets.com

ChooseFI is a website, podcast and growing community focusing on financial independence (FI). Entries include interviews and articles on how to save, invest and retire early. ChooseFI.com

Afford Anything is a fabulous podcast by Paula Pant. As her introduction states, "You can afford anything, but not everything." I love this woman and her clear explanations of all things financial. Affordanything.com

Rich Dad Poor Dad by Robert Kiyosaki changed the way I think about work and finances. Simply put, he advises that developing investments and assets is the way to grow wealth, and that breaking out of the hamster wheel of salary-based earnings is the key to financial growth.

From those I've met on the road, here are some of the ways people have financed their travel:

Saving

Saving is so important. It can pay for our homes and our retirement, and can save us financially in emergencies. Money buys us time. It can also pay for our travel. Regardless of what one earns, saving is a skill that can be developed. A first step is being aware of what you spend.

To begin exercising your saving muscle, start a list or spreadsheet of where your money is going. See if there are places to cut. Do you eat out many nights a week? Do you need that much clothing or the newest electronic gadget? Do you need subscriptions to EVERY movie streaming service? Do you buy a new car when a used one will suffice? Once you've seen where you can cut, make a fund for travel and put money in there every week, whether it's a dollar or a thousand dollars.

Selling everything

Many families sold their homes and all their belongings in order to fund their travels. Savings from a house sale can last for years overseas depending on your spending habits. Many travelers used the sale monies to begin traveling in comfort, then looked for online work years into the journey.

Rentals

If you'd rather keep your home for when you return, you can rent out rooms or the entire house. I wrote earlier about using one's home for leverage and "house hacking."

Income from property rental, if you're lucky enough to have it, may still not be enough to cover living expenses when you travel. Many will need to work on the road. If that's your situation then before you travel, you'll need to review your options. If you're working full time and love your job, you can ask your boss if you can do it remotely. If COVID taught us one thing it's that remote work is entirely possible. You may want to try a short-term trip to see if remote work is really viable. If your office requires that you to come in once a week, you might try shorter trips within the country. You can find listings of full and part time remote jobs on sites like flexjobs.com, remotewoman.com or indeed.com.

The Side Hustle

There are so many different and creative ways that people make money on the road. Here is just a short list of what some people are doing to support themselves while traveling:

-Astrology readings (also tarot cards, palm reading, etc.)
-Blogging, including guest blogging
-Baking cookies
-Building apps, websites, designer
-Career counselor

-Computer help

-Creating content

-Customer support

-Day trading

-Digital marketing

-Dog walking

-Dropshipping. This has become very popular with travelers, particularly because you don't need a physical storage space. Find unique items to sell and do it all electronically. Check out sites like dropshiplifestyle. com to learn the way.

-Editing and copywriting. Outlets like Freedom from Writing offer courses and submission possibilities.

-Home-based travel agency

-IT consulting

-Journalism, writing articles on travel, motherhood, entrepreneurship, etc.

-Life coach

-Massage therapist

-Outschool, teaching. Just one of many platforms for online classes.

-Photography business, online and offline, including weddings, family portraits, animals.

-Podcasting

-Real estate investing

-Relocation services

-Renting out a decorated campervan as a photo booth

-Selling art online

-Search engine evaluator

-Selling products (often MLMs)

-Selling jewelry

-Selling on Ebay (clothing, shoes, electronics)

-Social media manager – helping individuals and businesses with daily posts, managing their messages, increasing followers with hashtag methods.

-Teaching English. The most popular outfits have included VipKid (vipteachers.com), whose primary audience is in Asia and specifically China, and goodairlanguage.com. There's also GogoKid, Cambly, Qkids, SayABC, Magic Ears, Lingoda, Dada and others.

-Teacher training and assessing

-Teaching an online course, from business to real estate to painting. I've seen courses on side hustles, building your remote business, or finding remote working gigs and how to travel.

-Teletherapy (psychotherapy and counseling done online)

-Virtual Assistant - Offering administrative services, including scheduling, phone calls, travel arrangements or managing email accounts, to clients from a remote location. You can market your skills on sites like Fivrr, Upwork or on various Facebook pages.

-Writing articles and books

And many more...

One useful recommendation from fellow traveler Tracey Tullis is to try to define and establish your new hustle (or occupation if this is more of career change than added hustle), *before* you hit the road.

"The only thing I would do differently would be to learn a translatable skill like becoming a virtual assistant before we left as opposed to while we were traveling. It worked out, but it was a tremendous amount of work that could have been avoided had we done some due diligence before we left."

Save on Travel Once You're on the Road

Be sure to sign up for websites that advertise cheap flights or flight specials. My favorite remains Scott's Cheap Flights (scottscheapflights.com). They are especially good at listing flights priced in error. An airline must honor the listed price, even if it is an error, at least and until the error is corrected. These tickets go quickly as an airline will correct the error as soon as it is discovered.

Hopper.com allows you to plug in a route and gauge when the highest and lowest prices of the month or year may be. Skyscanner.com, expedia.com and orbitz.com are go-to resources for many travelers searching for flights. Note that Tuesdays are said to be the best time to look for a flight, and clearing one's computer cache often produces better flight prices. Even groupon.com sometimes offers short getaways for affordable prices.

Another way to save on travel costs is not to travel by air or train at all. Eurovelo is one of many different options for exploring Europe by bicycle (eurovelo.com). There are eight routes that crisscross Europe with names like Pilgrims Route, River Route, and Sun Route. Each offers a different vista, experience, and difficulty level. There are also travel experiences to be had on foot, like walking the Camino de Santiago in Spain or the Appalachian Trail in the United States.

Once you're in country, local airlines can offer great deals and generally are much less expensive. Ryanair.com offers dirt cheap flights within Europe; the catch is that you must be spontaneous and have little or no luggage. But for families with a base who want a quick week in a nearby country, the cost savings can be immense. These seemingly great deals can also come with hiccups. The Mexican airline volaris.com has been known to spontaneously cancel or change flights with little or no warning. The message here is: do your research. List-serves are an especially good source for this information.

Often an airline will require you to have a round-trip ticket before you are allowed to board. For many families starting out on a world adventure, this can be impossible if a family has no idea when they are returning nor from which country they might return home. A creative solution is offered by Air Onward Ticket, an online company that will let you rent a ticket for $8. If a round-trip ticket is required, go to their website aironwardticket.com and rent a return ticket for a few bucks. The rented ticket is only good for 36 hours but it should do the job.

Alternative Modes of Transport

One couple took a "repositioning cruise" from Spain to Brazil. These are usually one-way itineraries used to relocate a cruise ship from one region to another, and often include paying passengers. The company this couple chose, Costa Cruises, catered to Brazilians returning home and had a reputation as a party barge. If that's your style, check out vacationstogo.com and look for their selections on repositioning. The site has a vast selection not only of cruises but safaris and resort packages.

There are also similar relocation services for Recreational Vehicles, whereby some companies will pay you to transport their vehicles to a certain location. This sometimes include gas money or the possibility of extending your drive beyond the location or timeframe requested. Be sure to check if there are restrictions, such as mileage limits, route restrictions or other, and whether insurance is included or whether you will need to insure yourself. Information sites include lmoova.com or the Pan American Travelers Association Facebook page, which often requests help relocating vehicles. Outdoorsy.com is one RV Rental service, rvezy.com is another. For relocating basic automobiles, a popular outfit is Auto Driveaway (autodriveaway.com). Another is parsinc.com.

Turo is a site that lets individuals rent out their personal vehicles, often at significantly lower prices than rental agencies. One traveler recommended getaround.com, which rents cars by the hour, and which was just beginning to expand in the US.

More common transport options include Uber and Lyft, which remain popular throughout the world. In some countries the service only allows three people to ride at once. In Southeast Asia Uber was acquired by a company called Grab.

Many people choose to get an international driver's license, which is available through AAA in the US. If you think you might rent a car, travelers advise you get your license several months before you leave and not when you are already abroad.

In addition, for those renting cars in foreign countries, be sure to see if the credit card with which you rent the car also covers accident insurance. Travelers have reported being gouged by agencies whose insurance charges and other fees have far surpassed the cost for the rental car itself.

Carpooling service BlablaCar is popular in Europe, and connects drivers with passengers who are heading in a similar direction. The name comes from their rating service that ranks one's chattiness from Bla, Blabla, to three Blas for those who just won't shut up. The website is: blablacar.com

At last report, the platform had more than 90 million users and was being used in about 22 different countries. Sadly, the service has no plans to come to the United States. Still, Blablacar continues to grow in other regions of the world. For those still willing and eager to share a ride, this is a great and practical service.

Pan American Travelers Association is directed towards overland travelers on the American continent who want to connect with others. There are lots of questions about border crossings and dangers, and there are requests for great stopping spots, best internet services, interactive maps, plus calls for people to share a shipping container to cross the Darién Gap to South America (The Gap separates the North and South American continents and can only be crossed by boat as the jungle is dense and there is no road). There also are many vehicles for sale. The Pan American Facebook page often shares dreamy pics of these outfitted rigs, both funky and in states of sublime perfection.

Saving Money with Credit Cards

I've mentioned sites that offer great flight deals. Another way to get reduced or free flights is through credit card points. In fact, people get very serious about "credit card hacking." I met a woman at a travel conference who had just flown round trip from Florida to Peru because a recent credit card special earned her twice as many miles for the flights. I couldn't believe my ears. This is a long flight and she had no intention of seeing anything in Lima, Peru; she was flying these long legs only to garner more airline miles.

Another mom told me she had sixteen different credit cards, several of which offered mileage bonuses for signing up. Some airline credit cards also get you free checked bags and priority boarding. Others offer access to a VIP lounge, which for long flights can be a blessing. There are numerous tips and strategies out there on transferring points around for maximum redemption value. One of the best sites for all things credit card is thepointsguy.com. Check out his website which explains everything there is to know about maximizing all the benefits of credit card points. @milesmom also gives pointers on great deals and strategies for receiving flight miles. Familiesflyfree.com has some excellent suggestions on how to accumulate enough points so families can, as the title suggests, fly free all around the world. Don't forget cash back offers, most of which are listed at the cashbackmonitor.com.

There are apps that can organize your credit cards, even taking note of your sign-up date and notifying you when you're eligible for new bonuses. Awardwallet.com, for example, lets you track frequent flyer miles and hotel points and book reward tickets. Points.com is another favorite.

A word of caution about credit cards: gathering points can offer wonderful rewards, but please be responsible and pay your bills off each month. The interest on credit card debt is a silent drain on your finances that builds and builds. Use credit cards wisely – not as a substitute for actual money (that you may not have), but as a temporary tool that helps you buy the things you need. In fact, if you wouldn't pay for it with cash, do not pay for it with a credit card. Be aware also that each credit card or credit application can lower your overall credit score. A lower credit score can impact your ability to borrow money from a bank.

Accessing Money Abroad

Whether you're working from the road or living from savings, you'll need to access your money while traveling. Using your credit cards to get cash at an ATM is a convenient way to get cash, but foreign transaction fees add up fast. A debit card is far superior and doesn't incur interest charges as credit cards do, but it usually incurs the same withdrawal fees. I recommend a Schwab account with a debit card (schwab.com/checking). It's one of the few accounts I'm aware of, along with some credit unions, that will reimburse your ATM fees at the end of every month. These fees are usually quite low — about $2.00 a transaction — but if you're traveling for a while, or making frequent trips to the ATM, those small amounts add up. Having it all reimbursed is a nice feature. Foreign banks also will charge a fee so you want to avoid being charged twice for one transaction. I also advise traveling with some emergency cash in case you have difficulties at any point with your card. Please note that you'll get the best exchange rates by using your card at an ATM, not on the street or at a kiosk.

One last word on money and a journaling exercise

I love talking to my friends about money. I love breaking down finances and helping people explore where they are spending and how they might make money in different areas, like house hacking. But talking about money makes some people very uncomfortable. Some of us — and I will include myself in this group — were brought up not to talk about money. In my family it was considered vulgar and made them suspicious, as if I were trying to find a way to take it from them. I was led to believe I would inherit at least a bit from my wealthy grandmother, but when she died I received not one cent. This made me smarter and more savvy, as I was forced to focus on my financial future and think through how my older years might look. I'm trying to raise my son so he feels comfortable talking about money and that he thinks about ways to save and plan while he's still young — whether that includes travel or other goals.

I like to think of money as a tool that allows you to build a life you want. If the tool doesn't work well, what are some ways to sharpen it to help you achieve your goals?

Take some time now to think specifically about how you might finance a life of travel.

I asked earlier if you had a remote job. If not, could you ask to work from home or remotely? Now let's dive deeper.

Could you comfortably cut back on hours or would you need to work full time?

Are you in a job where you could take paid or unpaid leave or a sabbatical?

How do you feel about quitting?

Do you have savings? If not, can you find ways to cut back on your spending to build a travel fund?

Can you create other streams of income, for example, by taking a summer job or freelancing?

What are your talents?

Can you house hack?

What bills would you need to pay while you're on the road?

How much can you automate?

What would you do with your pets? Can you take them with you? Can you leave them with family? Find a long-term placement? Or should you get a housesitter (which means you may not be able to rent out your house)?

The point of journaling through these questions is to get you thinking about where your money is going and how you might rearrange your physical and financial life to create more possibility.

In Egypt, our group of family travelers
explored by dune buggy.

Tracey, Rob and Makai Tullis

In Search of a Family-Friendly Culture

"The only thing I would do differently would be to learn a skill that was transferable before we left as opposed to while we were traveling."

That's the advice from Tracey, who began traveling with her husband Rob, and their son Makai, when their son was five. The Canadian couple initially lived off savings and had no translatable skills for online work. They eventually learned to work online – Rob as a Wordpress expert and Tracey a Virtual Assistant – but it wasn't without challenges.

"People have said, 'we're going to go and take what we have saved and not worry about budget, and figure it out while we're on the road.' It's very difficult to try and figure it out when you're also researching travel arrangements, where to book accommodation, and all the other things that come along with travel. So yes, definitely work on budget and planning, but also prepare for consistent income."

From Calgary, Alberta, the couple were always drawn to travel. Once Makai was born, they struggled with decisions about whether both parents would work, or whether one could stay home, which is what they preferred. Neither wanted daycare.

"*We* wanted to raise our son, or at least have one of us at home," Tracey said. "But the cost to do that when we were living in Canada was too much. Something had to give."

They'd been reading about other families who'd sold their homes and traveled the world when it hit them that they could do that too and travel during Makai's growing years. Once they made the decision, it didn't take long. "We quit our jobs, sold everything, and left," she said.

They began their journey in Colombia, attracted by a family-friendly culture in a location that might not be as overrun with tourists. Both parents felt family focus was lacking in their home culture and the fact that travelers were still intimidated by Colombia's violent past, didn't deter them. In fact, for Tracey fewer tourists was a positive.

In the beginning, having quit their jobs in Canada, they lived off money from the sale of their home. Once they started traveling, they decided learning remote skills would be the best way to extend their journey. That's when Rob became a Wordpress expert and Tracey trained to be a VA, which is currently one of the fastest-growing opportunities for remote work.

Their biggest fears before traveling hadn't been about work; rather, they were worried about their lack of any foreign language skills. Over time, they realized that this wasn't such a barrier; in many instances, it opened doors. Tracey said they had to figure out ways to express themselves to get things done, which was challenging, but ultimately rewarding. It pushed them to learn enough to get by in each country.

"People worked to connect with us and it helped us get outside of our comfort zones," she said.

Makai watched TV in a variety of countries and like many children was able to absorb languages much faster than his parents. He is homeschooled by both parents, with his learning based loosely on the Canadian curriculum, which is available online. Rob's mom was a primary teacher for 25 years, so the couple said they had lots of support. Having never been in a public school, Makai's interactions on the road also became the foundation on which he built his blossoming social skills.

"He had no preconceived notions that people wouldn't like him. He wasn't afraid to go and engage, even though he knew people couldn't understand him. He never hesitated," Tracey said. "I think he's very confident and independent now. [Four years into their travels] and he doesn't have a problem entering a large group of people he doesn't know and immediately starting to mix."

The family traveled through Europe – Spain and Romania were the best for children, places where "kids could be kids," she said – then drove an RV through Mexico. They weren't able to do home exchanges since they had sold their home, but house sitting accounted for roughly two years of free accommodation out of their four years of travel. Tracey said housesitting changed the way they traveled and made it far better.

"We got to know locations – the best restaurants to eat, and the best attractions to visit – because home-owners would tell us. You'd get a local's opinion and a local who's not trying to sell you something," she said. "Housesitting really enriches travel and changes how affordable it can be for you."

The couple uses both <u>trustedhousesitters.com</u> and also <u>housecarers.com</u>, both of which offer extensive international house sits. They specifically chose house sits with pets because they missed their own dog, which stayed behind with family, but there are plenty of options without pets. People simply need others to watch their homes, particularly if they're leaving for an extended period. Their need is your opportunity.

Tracey's last words of advice were not to be swayed by naysayers.

"If it's something you feel is a good move for your family, don't let anybody talk you out of it. One thing we experienced a lot of was opposition. I know other families who have as well, even those who hadn't planned to travel for as long as we had. Second, don't let things hold you back, like language, if that's a concern for you. We were blown away by how that is just not anything to worry about."

Essential Travel Items

The first is headlamps (and extra batteries!), because power outages are something we experienced in every country we visited.

The other is a Scrubba wash bag. It is the most amazing travel thing I have ever owned. It's essentially a dry bag with a nubby little washboard on the inside that you fill with water. You could put five things in at a time and your laundry soap and you roll it like a dry bag and then there's a stopper you pull out. It gets stuff cleaner than a washing machine, I'm not joking. It's worth its weight in gold and it's so light. More like 10 times its weight in gold!

Chapter 21

Some Necessities for Remote Working

There are so many possibilities for earning income through remote work, but they all have one thing in common: the need for good and consistent WiFi. This rules out some locations, though fewer every day.

In locations where there is no WiFi, it's often easiest and cheapest to buy a country-specific SIM card when you arrive. You can find these at airports, and at corner stores like a *Tabac* in France or a *papeleria* in Latin America.

For shorter trips you can also ask your carrier about their international plans. I chose GoogleFi (fi.google. com) as my primary phone service as it allows me to have instant phone usage and WiFi access in each country if those trips are under three months (their limit). This saves me time and frustration and allows me to hit the ground running. For an additional $15 my son has service on his phone as well.

Hotspots: Companies like Travelwifi.com offer portable hotspot units with a range of price plans, including daily rental.

Small, portable internet boosters are also popular, particularly when you have WiFi, but it may not be strong enough or reach every room in your accommodation. They're small enough to pack and can ensure adequate connection even through thick walls. The wireless router I purchased is the GL.iNet pocket-sized hotspot, but there are many others.

Starlink satellite broadband is one mobile internet solution that is gaining popularity with overlanders. Engineered by SpaceX, it uses advanced satellites in low orbit to enable internet access in areas with low to no broadband. However, Starlink's cost is comparatively steep at nearly $600 for equipment and more than $100 a month for the subscription fee. As time goes on, I would expect more and easier satellite connections.

Chanel Morales

Take it Online!

"I just decided I was going to do it!"

Most the people I meet on the road had some level of fear before starting their travels, especially single mothers. Chanel was not one of these people. Chanel is an early 30-something single mom from England who decided in 2018 to take her eight-year-old daughter out of school and start traveling the world. Her own mother, also a single parent, had done the same, taking Chanel to Australia when she was only six. Her grandmother did the same. "I've only ever seen single moms and they all traveled." Fear of travel was simply not in the mix, especially not in English-speaking countries.

With a background in digital marketing and social media management, she had long realized that a 9-to-5 job was "not fun," she said. Given that her job was already location independent – albeit with a monthly income of only £1000 a month (close to $1,200) – she decided to jump. "I just decided I was going to do it."

She researched flights via skyscanner.com, which she swears by, with the goal of going the furthest for the lowest amount. Behold: a one-way ticket to Boston, MA for £150. "I didn't think about the fact that I was flying to another expensive country. I didn't go to Asia, or somewhere equally inexpensive, like a smart person would have done."

"I had a whole £300 in my bank account the day I left. I flew to Boston with three nights booked in Airbnb, and a flight from LA two months later."

She toured some of the larger East Coast cities, then moved south and west across the country, where she stayed with Worldschooling families she'd met online.

"I posted on Facebook, 'I'm going to be traveling the world with my daughter. Does anyone want to meet up?' The Americans are so hospitable they all invit-ed me to come stay with them. They all gave me a room with ensuite bathroom. Your houses are big over there!"

For a year the duo did Workaways (workaway.info) and housesitting "on an absolute shoestring" while Chanel was building her business. She launched a coaching business a year into her travels and was quickly successful. That meant leveling up her accommodations – more Airbnbs and fewer homestays. Though it was nice to have their own space and easier to get work done, Chanel said she missed the connection to people, and the deeper cultural understanding she got in those communal situations.

They began their travel in part as a response to an educational system Chanel said was not supportive of her daughter's learning struggles: she had dyslexia and was unable to read. Once they hit the road and the pressures of traditional school were removed, reading suddenly came much easier.

Their first year was spent slowly traveling and doing some school lessons throughout the week, though veering away from traditional curriculum. They had context-driven conversations about the areas they visited, like the Martin Luther King Memorial in Washington, DC, and the site of the Salem witch trials.

As they travelled, her daughter also learned a lot of her mother's entrepreneurial spirit and skill. "She knows the lingo — terms like niche marketing," Chanel said.

"At the end of the day, she'll know how to make money, and that's why we want our kids to work, right? We want them to get an education so they can get a good job so they can make money. Well, I'll just skip all that and say, this is how you make money, and just cut out the middle man." Chanel also celebrates the deeper values and skills her daughter has learned from travel: her understanding of other cultures, her flexibility, her emotional intelligence, and her confidence to approach and meet new people.

"She's worldly wise and doesn't have that small-minded mentality one has when you've grown up in one place and you only see things from one perspective. She sees things from lots of different perspectives and is very understanding of people because of that. Those things formed her personality."

Perceiving what others need is what propelled Chanel onto a new level of remote work. By the end of 2021 she had created a six-figure business coaching others on how to start and launch online businesses. It's about having freedom, she tells her clients. Not only to travel, but to be with your kids, to take care of your health or whatever other needs arise. She described some of her key lessons:

"Surround yourself with people already doing it, because that will generally wipe away most of your fears. I've seen this single mom with three small children, and she's traveling everywhere. Just being in the World-schooling groups will show you that it's possible."

Then set your intention. For example, if you make a friend who lives in Mexico set an intention to go visit them – then it's not as scary. You're not going to be alone, because you know somebody in that place. That's my practical advice.
In terms of mindset, you can create a vision board and get really focused on the things you want to see. Let your brain start to feel that it's a reality, and start to set the course in motion for those things to become reality for you."

Chanel and her daughter will head out traveling again soon – it's in their DNA, she says. He favorite location is Turkey, with its Middle Eastern energy and European comforts. "The food is amazing, the people are so friendly. It's just an incredible place." One thing she won't do again is take a Greyhound bus in the US, which she recalls as a disastrous 24-hour experience of inefficiency, dirt, and discomfort. Coming from Europe's far more developed transport systems, the shock of North America's substandard public transport has yet to wear off.

Her final words of advice for those contemplating travel?

"You can never lose anything by traveling. I mean, you can lose things a lot of the time, but you never really lose anything if it's a lesson. No matter what happens, even if something goes wrong. Probably my worst experience – on a Greyhound bus in America – was traumatic, but I definitely learned something from that experience. I think all the things that go wrong are lessons, and you only ever come out wiser and smarter, and it's just a beautiful thing, so go for it. Do it no matter what."

Essential Travel Items

A wash bag for clothing items.

A tripod for online and video work.

An adjustable and compact computer platform for varying workspaces in hotels and homes around the world.

A Brief Coaching Class on Making Money Online

Chanel runs masterclasses and courses teaching people how to make money online using their own skill set. She shared some of the important lessons:

It's important to spend time thinking about your current skills. A lot of us assume that to make money online, we must retrain, take a course, or get a certification, and that's not the case. Everyone has knowledge and skills already. It might be something that you don't realize is important, or that other people don't know. You might be really good at editing, or having a healthy diet, or you might be really good at parenting your children. There are so many things that you probably already do well that you could turn into a business.

There are six business models that I highly recommend because they're very easy to get started. The financial barriers to entry are minimal, and they can scale to millions in income. Those are:
coaching
online courses
membership sites
digital marketing
agency consultancy
virtual assistant work

Most people can find something to apply to one of them. Whether you create a membership site showing people how to become vegan, or you create a coaching course on how to lose weight, or become a VA and help people with social media, there's something for everyone.

The other piece of advice is: don't go out there trying to sell something low value, like an e-book that's $10. If you think logically, how many of those will you need to sell to make $5k a month? You must have a massive audience, and the fact is that most people won't have a massive audience in the beginning. Sell one thing that's expensive, and you can make money a lot quicker. For example, a coaching program. A 12-week coaching program could be anything from $1,000 to $10,000, depending on the transformation. The word "transformation" is key.

Think about the transformation you can create for someone. What point A to point B could you take someone through? People don't really care about what you can do for them; they care about their own transformation. Figure out how, with what you know, you can change someone's life. Then you can sell it for whatever price you want.

Chanel adds that people who are successful managing multiple streams of income likely didn't start them all at once. So if you have many ideas, focus in on one at a time. Get really good at one thing first, before adding other ideas.

Paul Carlino

Don't Forget your Taxes!
(Because your taxes will never forget you)

Me: So I just paid state taxes for four years when I didn't need to?
Paul: Absolutely.
Me: Sigh... that's why I wrote this book.

After health insurance and medical concerns, the next dreaded inevitability might be taxes. You can't escape them – even if you're planning on traveling the world, and especially if you plan on creating a remote work life. What you may not know is that your taxes could be far less than you anticipated. I spoke to former IRS tax attorney Paul Carlino to find out what American expats should know about their tax liabilities. The takeaway: don't just forget about the IRS when you've left the country, because the IRS never forgets you.

Paul is a 50-something retired tax attorney living in San Miguel de Allende, Mexico. He worked for 20 years with the Office of Chief Counsel, a department of attorneys within the Internal Revenue Service, including some time in the international tax division. Then in 2018 he and his wife decided to leave the country with their two children. They settled in central Mexico where Paul began helping expats with their tax returns.

The first thing that's important for people to know is that when you leave the US, as a US citizen, you don't stop paying US taxes. The US taxes worldwide income, whether you live and earn money in Mexico, Massachusetts or Malta.

The most important part of the US tax code for every expat — meaning those who truly live overseas — is the foreign earned income exclusion. This provision allows you to exclude up to a certain amount of earned income each year from taxation. Earned income means money that you earn for your work, whether you're an employee or self-employed. In 2022 that threshold was about $112,000, and it is adjusted each year for inflation. You claim the foreign earned income exclusion on Form 2555, which you attach to your Form 1040, the basic tax form.

Note: this is an exclusion related to your income tax. The exclusion does not apply to Social Security tax and Medicare, he said. But first: a bit more on this foreign earned income exclusion.

In order to qualify for the Foreign Earned Income Exclusion, your "tax home," which is where you primarily live and work, needs to be in a foreign country. You also need to meet one of two residency tests: the first is a bona fide resident, meaning that you were in the foreign country on January 1, and you were there for the whole year. Under this test you can take short trips out of the country, including to the US. But your intent always needs to be that you're going back to the foreign country because that's where your home is.

If you don't meet the bona fide residence test, you can satisfy the physical presence test; it works best for people traveling through multiple countries. That requires more than 330 days of travel in a twelve-month period, and it's very exact. Three hundred and twenty-nine days doesn't qualify. Then, of course, you have to have earned income.

You can qualify under either test year to year; Paul and his family spent a year driving through South America and used the physical presence test. Then they settled in Central Mexico on January 1 and used the bona fide residence test.

Another important point Paul brought up is that people may not need to file state returns if they're not living in the US. "A lot of people still file a state tax return in the state where they used to live, even though they're now living in Mexico or some other foreign country. That may not be necessary. If you don't live in a state, then you are a nonresident of that state. Generally, states only tax nonresidents on income that is sourced in that state. If you don't have any income from that state, you don't need to file a state tax return. For example, when we lived in Virginia, we were taxed by Virginia on all of our income. However, when we moved to Mexico, we were not residents of Virginia. We still owned a house there, but we rented it. We file a Virginia nonresident tax return, which reports our Virginia rental income, but not our investment income or the income we earn in Mexico. That income is not sourced in Virginia. So you can save a lot of money by not filing a state tax return if you don't live there and have no state sourced income."

A lot of the people I've met on the road stopped paying taxes — a bad idea, as we've noted, because the government keeps track of you. If you earn income, they've got a record of that, and if you don't report it and pay any tax due, you're accruing interest and penalties. So file your taxes. The IRS has a three-year period of limitations where they can challenge someone who's filed a return. If you never file a return, then you haven't started that period of limitations running.

On the plus side, people can be eligible for credits, like the stimulus payments the government distributed during COVID-19. If you didn't receive that payment, you can put it on your return and receive those monies as a refundable credit. Even if you lived out of the US, you were still eligible to receive those payments. Families traveling with children under the age of 17 can also take advantage of the child tax credit, which will reduce any tax they owe.

This information is for general educational purposes only and you should always consult an accountant about your specific circumstances and payment needs.

CONNECT

During our group trip to Bali one of the
parents gave a lesson about volcanoes.

Chapter 22

Travel Smarter

Sustainability and Cultural Sensitivity on the Road

One year my son and I joined a Worldschooling group trip to Indonesia, which included an incredible scuba and boat trip to watch the manta ray migration. The area is known as one of the most biodiverse and nutrient rich areas, and every year thousands of these immense gentle creatures pass through. I will never forget the moment of dropping into the water to see a school of massive rays swimming below me. It felt like a religious experience.

As I continued watching them swim, arching to the surface in search of food, I saw that the waters were filled with plastic cups and bags that the rays were mistaking for jellyfish. I wanted to scream at them to stop, to close their mouths or the floating plastic would kill them.

For the rest of the trip, we collected bags of garbage from the beach and waters. We picked up bottles and cups, clothing and baskets, and so many straws. It felt like the smallest effort in a literal sea of garbage. The experience devastated me and I still carry the weight of our human responsibility and consumerist destruction.

Travel has an impact, wherever we go and however long we stay. Our responsibility is to make that impact more good than bad. In an article on people's return to travel post COVID, adventure guru Rick Steves told the *New York Times* that travel was "a powerful force for peace and stability on this planet."

"What you want to do is bring home the most beautiful souvenir, and that's a broader perspective and a better understanding of our place on the planet — and then employ that broader perspective as a citizen of a powerful nation like the United States that has a huge impact beyond our borders," he told the Times.

I agree with this wholeheartedly. The point of this book is to encourage people not simply to travel, but to travel for the greater educational and cultural impact that it provides. That means bringing sensitivity to your interactions and education to the ways you move through the world.

There are specific ways to travel smarter.

One of our greatest carbon footprints comes from air travel, so one of the best ways to cut back on those emissions is simply to fly less. Ironic, I know, considering this is a book about travel. But I bring you back to the idea of slow travel, to spending more time in each place and taking a deeper dive into the cultures you are visiting. Take a walking tour, support local merchants rather than larger chains and restaurants, and organize homestays to support residents.

While many travelers have moved by cruise ship, these vessels are particularly bad; the amount of pollution they leave in the ocean is truly shocking. Not only do ships emit double the carbon dioxide of flying, but their emissions harm marine life. There are few ways to have no impact at all, but there are choices you and your powerful spending can make.

One of the themes in this book is that travel teaches us to live with less. For example, when my son and I travel we take public transport, we shop for fresh foods and do our laundry only when we really need to, taking care to use little water if we're doing it ourselves. Travel teaches us to pare down and focus on the basics. I think it makes us better people – and more aware stewards of our environment.

Throughout the world, there has been a rise in sustainable and eco-friendly experiences, like eco tours in the jungle of Costa Rica or in the countryside of Eastern Europe, where bicycles are a common form of transportation. There are travel agents whose expertise is sustainable tourism; by supporting these businesses, you are supporting a larger philosophy that says that being sensitive to the environment has an economic value. I'd encourage everyone reading this book to put your dollars toward a sustainable, enriching world. Note: please dig a bit to make sure these tours are indeed eco-friendly: do they support local merchants? Does the tour have a light footprint? What about it is sustainable? etc. There is an increasing amount of "green washing" – claiming to be sustainable without actually being so – in pursuit of tourist dollars. Try your best to make sure your money is truly furthering sustainable practices.

Pack with sustainability in mind

If you're heading to an ocean or reef, research sunscreen that doesn't have harmful chemicals like oxybenzone. Carry your own stainless steel water bottles and ask for refills of water (though some restaurants and locations only offer plastic water bottles, so the other option is simply to drink beer or other bottled sodas). One family I saw had each child carry his own CamelBak, a backpack specifically for carrying water.

After walking along beaches in Indonesia strewn with garbage and plastic straws, I purchased stainless steel and bamboo straws so I could refuse plastic ones whenever offered. I gave these reusable straws to friends and made sure my son always had one on hand. I have a set of stainless steel camping cutlery; reusable plastic and bamboo sets are increasingly available. I carry my own containers for food and snacks to avoid plastic bags, and purchased a bamboo toothbrush after seeing so many plastic ones littering the beaches in Bali. Because tampons in foreign countries are only available with plastic applicators, I started researching alternatives. The Mooncup – a silicone menstrual cup – was my sanitary option of choice, though it does require water for rinsing. If you bring tampons, try to make sure they have cardboard applicators. Thinx period underwear are also popular.

I also bring my own light tote bags (I have different sized Baggu bags) that serve as reusable grocery or beach bags. And I travel with a fast-drying towel and rechargeable batteries.

For reading and entertainment, most people now carry a Kindle instead of paperback books, which lightens your load and allows for more reading options during your travels. (You can also use the Kindle app on your tablet or smartphone). There are also innumerable online travel games and apps.

New, sustainable options for travel emerge daily, and this too should be part of your research. We're trying to build a world where people travel to give back and not just to take and consume. Please join us.

One of my favorite travel stories is when I sent Aiden to get
me a birthday present in a busy market in Oaxaca, Mexico.
I gave him some money and sat down for a coffee. Minutes
dragged on and I started to panic that perhaps I had sent
him into danger, that he may have gotten lost — or been
abducted! I was about to approach a police officer when
Aiden rounded the corner with "my" birthday gift:
a hamster! The smile on his face made up for all my stress.
He was so proud of his accomplishment.

"Spike" stayed with us for the month then was
rehomed to a very happy little girl.

Astrid Vinji and Clint Bush

Making Travel Inclusive

"I wanted a place for people that had similar interests as me and specifically for people of color."

Clint and Astrid were lucky to encounter a group of Worldschooling families just as they were beginning to question their own life in Seattle. They both had 9-to-5 jobs, commuting into the office while their two young kids (eight and eleven at the time) were in childcare and school. As early as 2013, they began thinking about how to change their lives and do something entirely different. "Not only because of the level of stress, but because it felt so repetitive and monotonous," Clint said.

They heard about the Family Adventure Summit, a Worldschooling conference that was taking place in Penticton, British Columbia. They decided to drive north for the weekend, and without any expectations, listen to what Worldschooling was all about.

"At the conference we were just floored," said Clint. Presentations by long-time Worldschooling families, alongside hallway discussions and a dad's night out, allowed them to ask any and all questions they had about how to travel long term.

"We had a five-hour drive back to Seattle at the end of this conference and in that time we decided that this is what we wanted to do," Clint said. They set a goal to be on the road within nine months, which happened to be when the next Family Adventure Summit was taking place in San Miguel De Allende, Mexico.

The couple dove into logistical and personal planning. Both Astrid and Clint come from a project management background — Clint is a computer programmer and Astrid a program manager for non profits — so they quickly purchased software and began ticking items off their list, with check-ins every few weeks. They chose not to sell their Seattle house, and instead rented it out using a property management company.

"It was a process, and we tried to be very methodical about planning. Once we started actually purging stuff, I think that helped. We pared all of our clothing down to a suitcase while we were still living in the house."

Part of the planning process was financial. It helped that Astrid had always had a monthly budget for the family to keep track of expenses. Using their current budget as a starting point and incorporating the estimated costs of airfare and lodging, they projected they'd need $6000 per month. Clint would still need to work while Astrid could focus on schooling the kids.

One year on the road, and the budget needed to be revised. Astrid would need to work too if they were going to keep traveling. She eventually landed a fully remote job with a non-profit based in New York. The children's homeschooling would be shared; Clint taught math, Astrid helped with writing, and the kids did their independent work. Clint eventually returned to full time work as well.

With both parents working full time, it was difficult to juggle the tasks of childcare, teaching and travel organizing. They used time zones to their advantage, with European time zones working particularly well. For example, when they were in Spain, they could spend a full day as a family until 3pm, after which they'd work with the kids. Once they put the kids to bed, they'd begin their own workday, sleeping in the following morning.

Part of their strategy — which they described as "controversial" among Worldschoolers — is their dependence on technology, and a very flexible allowance of screen time. "The way we view it is that we do a lot of activities, so we feel like it's balanced between the activities they do, and the amount of screen time they get." It has also fostered a lot of interest: their daughter Mira watched YouTube videos on how to draw anime characters, which inspired her to make an anime movie on her phone. Julian got into coding, Minecraft and Roblox. Astrid explained how the week prior they had been in Grenada, Spain, walking on a street with a Moroccan feel. When Julian got back, he recreated that street in Minecraft, adding each store as he remembered it. "He was taking what he was experiencing and putting it into his own context," Astrid reflected.

The couple still budgets $6000 a month for their family of four. In countries like Mexico, Vietnam or Indonesia, they manage well with less than that; in other countries, the costs are higher. In Spain, for example, the cost of living was low, but they chose to rent a car and to live in a larger apartment so they could have ample work space during their three-month stay.

Having never homeschooled before, the couple said they were impressed by the practical skills their kids were learning every day. They've become adaptive and outgoing, and they integrate quickly and seamlessly with other Worldschoolers they meet while traveling. The kids engage with adults, and easily express themselves verbally. And they absorb bits of language, not with an immediate goal of becoming fluent, Astrid said, but as a means to develop an interest for possible future exploration.

"Each time we do lessons it's expanding their vocabulary, their knowledge and competence just a little bit more. I'm hoping that if they do decide to study Spanish more seriously, or Indonesian, or some other language, it will be easier for them, because they already have these word seeds planted in their brains."

Clint and Astrid are both South Asian — he is Filipino and she has Indonesian Heritage. Seeing how few families like theirs were traveling inspired Astrid to launch a Facebook group connecting and encouraging families of color.

Growing a community helps when sharing certain challenges, like the experience of microaggressions towards people of color who travel, particularly during the pandemic. They experienced both micro- and macro- anti-Chinese aggression in parts of Europe — particularly in Rome. Clint described a bus ride in Rome, with a fellow passenger grumbling anti-Asian insults throughout the ride.

"Those little moments we don't generally share with our Caucasian friends, largely because we're not exactly sure how aware they are. When other families of color are around, we don't need to explain the context to begin a conversation." Without similar shared experiences it can feel isolating, Clint said.

Astrid started another Facebook group about sustainable travel as she learned more about "the impact that we're making as travelers. Whether it's positive or negative, not just environmentally, but also culturally. I wanted to connect with other families who felt the same way, and maybe elevate the topic [of sustainability] to a more normal conversation within travel, instead of just this side topic."

She also wants to encourage families to go beyond surface travels and take time to learn about the cultures they're visiting, and to ask questions about why things are the way they are.

That level of communication and investigation is just as important within the family unit, she said.

"Travel has really helped us to be able to communicate with each other better. We still have our ups and downs, but we're a lot better at verbalizing, saying, 'This is how I feel right now.' Then we try and talk and recognize any problems before we start. If you discover those problems on the road, it's only going to make it worse."

"For us, it's made us stronger, but we we've had some friends who've had different outcomes over the years," she said, referring to a number of couples who decided to separate or divorce during their travels. "We know we can't let things fester, especially because we're living in small spaces. We have to be pretty vocal about what's bothering us. So just be prepared that traveling is going to bring up everything that you haven't really been addressing."

Astrid and Clint are impressive in many ways. Amid their full-time working, child educating and community building, the family also created and launched their own card game!

A graphic designer by training, Clint said he often re-designs things for his own purpose. After one such re-design, he realized how fun and simple it would be to design their own game.

"Mira and Julian and I just start brainstorming the idea right there." As a family, we're sitting there drawing the cards based on the concept. Once the cards were cut and the game concept in play, Astrid asked "What if we made it into a product and we sold it on Amazon?" They did just that. The game is called Scoops and is available on Amazon.

Essential Travel Items

An additional monitor, a wireless internet booster and a laptop lift to raise my computer for better viewing. Plus, an external keyboard and mouse. Each child has an iPad.

For schooling we have a map we picked up in Italy. We put it up in every place we land, making us feel more at home.

Dry erase sheets to put calendars and lists. We bring kitchen knives wherever we go, because invariably the Airbnbs have terrible kitchen knives. For organizing travel, we use a travel app called Clubhouse (not to be confused with the virtual meeting space). Also, notion.so, which is a site that allows you to have all your work in one place.

A French press so we can have good coffee.

We're trying to be much more aware of environmental impacts so we carry many sustainable items: we try and bring things that offset plastic bags, like tote bags for groceries and mesh produce bags. We use beeswax wraps to wrap food so we don't have to buy plastic wrap anymore.

The second thing we travel with is a Roku Ultra, which is very small. We plug that into the TV as soon as we get to a place. It has its remote and already has all of our streaming services set up. We connect it to internet, and we have our Netflix and Disney Plus (or whatever you use for streaming) already set up.

We also travel with a carbon monoxide detector, which I think saved us once in Mexico when the water heater was not vented properly. It's tiny, the size of our phone.

Then there's the family entertainment items: We have several card games that we bring everywhere, and of course our own game, Scoops.

The last thing is our ukulele! The whole family can play and learn on it and we've done jam sessions with other people.

Chapter 23

Relationships

While visiting with a group of world travelers recently, I was struck by the number of people wanting to discuss the difficulties of maintaining and nurturing one's relationships on the road. I shouldn't have been surprised. Relationships tend to be the most popular topics of discussion in almost any setting, so why wouldn't they be for families on the road?

For those aspiring travelers who are in partnerships, this chapter is for you.

Of *course* there are difficulties with relationships while traveling. In fact, any problem you might have at home only intensifies once you're on the road. For example, if you imagined that hitting the road for that round-the-world adventure was the way to save your marriage, then you're most likely going to be faced with deep disappointment. According to families who've been there, any squabble or tension will go on the road with you – only magnified, because you're spending every moment together, sometimes in very close quarters.

Those weeks when one partner failed to take out the garbage... that flirtatious look your spouse gave someone else... the disrespectful comment at the office party – it doesn't go away just because you've left home. Imagine being packed into in a car or shut in a shabby hotel room while it's pouring buckets outside. Now throw in a few anxious kids who are still a bit unsure about traveling, and maybe toss in a dog – or three cats (yes, I saw this). It can get really, really stressful. There are illnesses, language barriers, flat tires, days of boredom, crappy food, bad weather, whiney kids and fatigue – and those might be the good days! Bette Davis famously said, "Getting old ain't for sissies," and I'd say traveling isn't for sissies either. It's an endurance sport and you'd better be ready. In San Miguel de Allende there were so many separations, that my women friends and I wanted to start selling T-shirts that read, "I visited San Miguel and all I got was divorced."

Travel is not a panacea for a life that needs repair, and it won't make your problems go away. Travel won't fix a bad marriage or make a toxic work environment vanish. Wherever you go, there you are. So do the work and try to take care of any relationship problems before hitting the road. Put in the time and thought (and maybe find a virtual psychotherapist), and create a plan that works for you and your family. I write about travel not as a means of escape, but a path toward a better, richer more fulfilling life. It's not a vacation but a lifestyle. That lifestyle, if undertaken with intention, sensitivity and care, can help repair fractured relationships and bring families closer together.

First of all, make sure you agree on the *why* of your adventure, which should not be an attempt to salvage a struggling relationship. Establish yourselves as being fully capable of handling stress, disappointment and inevitable conflict in the most comfortable of circumstances, so you can handle these situations while traveling. Test the waters by starting with small adventures to see if you'll be great travel partners. If you haven't traveled together at all, then begin by planning a weekend away, then a week. This can be a good way to determine how you'll work through other problems you'll inevitably encounter on the road.

Most couples I've interviewed leave their homes, families, jobs and belongings, so they can have more family time. This doesn't mean couples should be attached at the hip, or that things will be perfect once you've finally left that stressful job. The truth is you'll get sick of each other, you'll question your decision possibly every day for months. You'll realize how little you can actually accomplish in a single day (particularly irritating for high-energy achievers), and you might even miss the familiar consistency of what you left behind, even if it was a job you disliked.

Know that you're on the right path. Find simple things to bring you joy. Go eat that ice cream cone that actually tastes like real cream, or see that movie – in English! – that your family has been wanting to see, and which just arrived in the Latin American city you're visiting. Be patient, with yourself and others. And most importantly, let go of wanting to recreate the style of living you left at home, and embrace what is new and different.

Here are some other tips for nourishing your relationship while traveling long term:

-Again, don't think that travel will heal a broken relationship. Please try to address significant issues *before* you hit the road.

-Take time together to connect at the end of the day or every few days, to review and reassess your strategies. Make a date night if your kids are old enough, or you've been in a place long enough to find reliable babysitters. Carve out time to remember what brought you together.

-As important as it is for each couple to find time together time, it's also essential that you find time to be alone and quiet. Being on the road can be a non-stop demand fest, particularly if your kids are hoping you'll substitute for the playmates they left behind. Add hours of driving in a cramped car and the feelings of strain can be potent. One traveling parent highly suggests the Relish app (hellorelish. com) for relationship enrichment. The book *Eight Dates: Essential Conversations for a Lifetime of Love* by John Gottman and Julie Schwartz Gottman also makes for great travel dates you can do again and again, including the absolute best step-by-step guide to resolving almost any conflict. "I swear it works," this traveler said.

-Some days make a decision to skip any cultural event you had planned in exchange for that green, leafy-treed park with a set of swings for the kids.

-Get out into nature. There are few things that an afternoon in nature can't improve.

-At the end of the day spend time remembering the fun or funny events, even if they didn't seem so funny at the time. Traveling — like relationships — demands a sense of humor. If you can't laugh at some of the crazy situations you will inevitably be faced with while on the road, then you might want to reconsider your decision to travel in the first place. Laughter, patience, and forgiveness will be critical tools for your trip — and for your life.

Shimea Hooks

Two-Mom Travel

Mea and her partner Cee launched into travel shortly after their son Caleb was born. "We [were] tired of spending more time with our coworkers than our family," they wrote on their blog itzafamilything.com. "Dogs spend more time with their puppies than mothers and fathers with their children... isn't it just heartbreaking?" With no paid maternity leave and childcare costs through the roof, the couple figured there had to be a better way. They decided to radically alter their life and travel the world.

They sold their San Diego, California, house then moved into a condo to save on expenses. Then a year later, just before leaving the country, they chose an extended stay hotel room where they didn't have to pay utilities, and which provided free breakfast and coffee.

"Our game plan was to try to save as much money as possible. After that, we just decided to go nomadic and that was it. We don't have a home base. We just love to travel."

Mea was well into her third year of full-time nomadic travel when I met her. Her motto at the time was to go "wherever the wind blows," including China, Singapore and Mexico. Their long-term plan was simply "to travel as long as we can with our son." Mea's partner Cee researches family-friendly locations, while Mea, a former teacher, spends a lot of time updating their blog about everything toddler and travel. They're also skilled at getting media and business sponsorship. In fact, they've managed to get quite a bit of financial support through affiliate programs and company partnerships. Sponsors recognize the value they provide for families who want to travel.

"Traveling with a kid can be overwhelming most of the time. So having the perfect products to go with you is everything. We write about things such as what breast pumps to take and their battery life, what icepacks you can travel with and to which countries, so you can actually get in and there's no problems with someone taking your breast milk. From snack containers to which strollers are good for hiking. Anything you can think of that's kid-related, we write about it. Even something as simple as mosquito repellent: which ones do you use for kids, which one can you use for yourself, or sunscreen that's reef safe. Anything you can think of, we try to make sure that we inform our readers about it."

Mea doesn't make a big deal about traveling as a lesbian couple with a child, nor has she had any difficulties with the issue. "We are very simple. We're not wearing pride shirts or anything. That's not a thing for us. We're just a happy couple who love one another who have a son. We're not in anybody's space trying to prove that we're gay and you have to like it. No one has ever really bothered us. I think they're more intrigued that there's black people in the neighborhood."

Instead, her challenges are about practical things, like the spike of prices for Airbnb and gas, or language barriers. But Google Translate can help travelers with almost anything, she says.

Luckily, their son has become quite the traveler.

"He loves plane rides. He knows that when he sits in the car that it's okay and I'll have activities made for him and all of those good things. I think it's just getting your kids used to making travels easy."

Her advice to other traveling families is to do your research. She recommends Facebook groups and talking to others with similar family make-ups or those traveling to similar places. She advises same-sex couples to be respectful.

"You're in someone else's space, so you kind of have to respect that and be careful. You don't have to be out and be affectionate. Be aware that other people don't feel the same way that you do. So just be safe."

The family has encountered other LGBTQ travelers by chance but not in any organized fashion. Mea admits she doesn't know many other lesbians out there doing what she's doing. But she'd like to encourage them all the same.

"Take a chance. You just never know what you don't know. Just take the jump. We were nervous about being two moms. We were nervous about being black. We were just nervous. You can always to go back and start over. In fact, you start over your whole life, whether it's a new job or a new neighborhood or a new apartment, so just jump. Start over."

Essential Travel Items

Cocoa butter. It's not just for moisturizing the skin. It's my baby oil or whenever my son has a bruise.

Beach bags. I use them for almost anything. It might be dirty clothes or groceries. Sometimes I'm over the weight limit for my luggage and I just put a couple of things in the bag and walk on the plane.

Chapter 24

Are You Ready?
A Journaling Exercise

By now I hope you feel more informed and more than a little bit inspired.

I'd like you to do a journaling exercise. Please think about the chapters you've read, the individual stories, and all the different ways people have chosen to travel.

Now think about the parts you've read that fit into your life, and perhaps the parts that don't. Imagine yourselves taking a leap into a life of travel.

What would it look like?

What's the absolute worst thing that you can imagine happening? What would your response be?

Consider those not-so-terrible but truly annoying things happening that you'd like to avoid. What would you do if they actually happened? How would it feel?

Now imagine the absolute best thing that could come out of traveling? What would that look like? How would you respond to it? Can you even imagine it?

How might your life change? Where are your children? Where is your marriage or your career? Where are your belongings?

Where are your deep friendships? Do you have any? Do have time for them?

Imagine yourself on your deathbed never having followed through on this desire. Would you have regrets? How would you have done it differently?

Review your answers and think deeply about what might first appear to be fears and limitations. Are they reasonable? At their worst, is it worth not taking a chance to travel? Do you have questions that still haven't been answered in some form?

If you need to talk through these fears, reach out to someone online. I'm certainly available for consultation. Re-read the stories of some of the travelers mentioned here. Most started with some level of fear and hesitation. Not one of them regretted his or her decision to travel with their family. Not one.

Sandra Odems

Sail Those Seas!

Sandra Odems and her husband bought a boat for $75,000 and left the country for a year with their three kids, aged seven, twelve and fifteen. They lived on savings while traveling — about $40-50k for the year — and once they returned sold the boat for the same price they'd paid. Both architects, they owned their own businesses, but chose to take the year off from work while traveling. The goal was family bonding, said Sandra, 50. The unexpected benefit was witnessing her kids' growing confidence, and their ability to better handle a variety of situations.

Her advice to others: Don't wait. Go before your kids are in high school. If finances are a concern, know that you can likely do it for a lot less than you think.

Essential Travel Items

A digital GPS.

Chapter 25

Friendships

I include a chapter on friendship because our friends have had the most lasting impact on my life and on that of my son. We now have cherished friends around the world and memories that will nurture us for years to come. We can't wait to meet up with these people again, somehow, somewhere.

In fact, social scientists have time and again observed that career, possessions, and wealth do not ultimately assure happiness. Friendships and family do.

Harvard professor Arthur Brooks writes frequently about the art and science of happiness, particularly in later life. His premise in the book *Strength to Strength* is that if you're only trying to accumulate money, prestige, power, pleasure, fame, and admiration, you're not going to be happy.

Brooks says that as people get older, they need faith, friendship, family, and a purpose in life. Many of us in middle age couldn't agree more. In fact, it's a common conversation among traveling families: having more time with family is the *why* of many of our adventures. What we find in travel is that our friendships also become much richer, especially at a time in our lives when new friendships can be more difficult to make. Our experience is that once we leave the confines of our 24/7 work life, we find lots more time for friends, and friends will have more time for us.

Before I left to travel I had more casual friends than I could see in any given week, but few of them had time for me. We scheduled weeks in advance for a coffee, which meant they couldn't really be counted on if I needed a friend that night. Americans in particular over schedule their lives to such an extent that a brief walk or a casual lunch has to be scheduled months in advance. An American friend I met in Mexico said she used to feel proud of this over scheduling, as if it reflected positively on her as a professional that she never had time for anyone.

I found that when we returned to the US for short or long spells, we were eager to reconnect with old friends. But many of those friends just didn't have time for us. I found myself more depressed than excited to be home. It was the same for my son: a simple play date had to be arranged weeks in advance, with last minute cancellations commonplace.

The travelers I've met on the road are some of the most creative, open-hearted and generous people I've ever met. Some of those I've met abroad and who remain on different corners of the globe, are my closest, dearest friends. They're the ones I call for support, with whom I share my struggles and my desires for future adventures. They're the ones who know by heart what it means to take a risk — and the benefits and hardships of doing so. I've found that these traveling friends have experiences that are similar and expansive enough to mine that they can support my fantasies and dreams, however foolhardy they might initially appear.

It's my experience that if I'm fantasizing about a new travel adventure, my friends at home might laugh or share all the reasons why such a trip is not workable. But travelers will start sharing all the possible ways to make that dream happen.

In fact I remember one such dinner party with some fellow world travelers who were about to head back to the US. We packed around a table holding large bowls of guacamole and chips, and yelled to each other over the mariachi music in the background. The conversation bounced from the confines of organized religion – two of the families present had had difficult partings from the Mormon Church – to travel. We covered best restaurants in our current Mexican location, education, work, and more. At one point, close to our lemon cheesecake dessert, I asked the group if they knew of any good animal sanctuaries that worked with elephants and that allowed children. Aiden really wanted to work with elephants. Because of our limited finances, we were thinking that Asia might be easier than Africa. Two of the families had in fact participated in elephant work, one at a wonderful sanctuary in northern Thailand, while others suggested ways to accomplish African safaris on a low budget (rent your own car and head out!). I scribbled pages of notes.

It occurred to me as I looked around the table, what an amazing community I had found. Not only could I ask about something as odd and *big* as wanting to go work with elephants, but it was considered a completely rational and normal request — in fact, they thought it was a great idea! Completely doable, and also very educational, they said. One friend chimed in with details: "The kids have to go into a giant closet where the food is stored and calculate, then carry out, the many tons of food the elephants will be eating during the day. No one is to ride them; that's the sign of an unethical sanctuary, as trainers have had to beat the animals into submission. So NEVER ride an elephant." I winced, remembering my elephant rides in Cambodia during my graduate work there. Back then I simply didn't know. I went home and looked up the suggested sites for elephant work and in a fit of spontaneity bought a ticket to northern Thailand for the following month. (We ended up having to postpone but it's still at the top of our bucket list.)

I have beloved friends around the world, but many of them might have laughed at my question. These friends often comment on why I don't just settle down, what I might be escaping, and wonder aloud where the money for *this* trip would come?

Interestingly, world-traveling communities most often tell you exactly where the money comes from. We are intent on building a community of digital nomads and otherwise location-independent colleagues and friends who share similar visions. We offer each other tips on work opportunities, suggestions on investments, property management techniques, and financial advisers. We talk about the highs and the lows of this life, because we are now all part of an informal family. Families that are each trying to make this very different way of living a bit more comfortable, and dare I say, mainstream. We advocate a kind of family-centered (however that family looks) larger worldview of education, travel, and engagement with societies different from our own. The goal is to build bridges and increase connections across cultures. Ultimately, we want a better, more thoughtful and kind world. We arrange to meet in different locations and discuss our educational strategies and inspirations whenever possible. We organize large play dates in parks, at local restaurants, or at Worldschooling conferences held around the world. If it sounds a bit utopist, well, in many ways it is. Our career goals are focused on creating a life that matters, while we have the energy to do so. Our response to naysayers is, "I am not escaping a life, but running toward and enthusiastically embracing a different one."

This lifestyle isn't always one big leap off a cliff into the unknown, even if it seems that way from afar. Many of these families have chosen to keep a home base, and most have extended family, which provides a measure of support for those inevitably long, tiring days on the road.

Many of us are making new families. Take the members of The Church of Jesus Christ of Latter-day Saints (Mormons) I mentioned earlier. When I asked about the most difficult part of leaving the Mormon Church, "Jeff" said it was the loss of a big Mormon family that stung the most. "Then we found this Worldschooling community and it became much easier," he said. "Now we have a new supportive family."

While I'm not part of any organized religion, I can deeply relate to the sentiment. For those of us who never really fit into a traditional or "normal" way of life, work, or schooling, it's refreshing to find others with a similar mindset. They're not social dropouts, though over the years I've certainly encountered that type too. The majority of travelers truly believe there is another way, and they're going to spend their lives making their chosen lifestyle a reality. They are the doers, the inventors, the investors and the creators, the curious and the educated, the manifesters and the inspired. I love these people, and I feel so fortunate to be learning from them every day.

About that month in Thailand? After being contacted by my French biological family, I decided it was more important to spend our funds and time visiting them in Europe, and reconnecting Aiden with cousins he hadn't seen in years. My new question is: with an extra week in Europe, where should we go? Rome and Pompeii? Greece and the Acropolis? Croatia? Paris, Paris, and more Paris?

Lainie Liberti and Miro Siegel

Helping Worldschooling Teens and Adults to Find Their Way

"Worldschooling made me a better parent, one hundred percent."

Lainie describes a very specific moment when she decided to leave everything and go traveling with her son. She was working late at her office in Los Angeles – a frequent occurrence for the single mother who ran a small design agency. Her 9-year-old son Miro sat nearby waiting for her to finish work. He had often asked her to work less and to spend more time with him, but supporting a child and living in America are costly and time consuming. Yet at that moment in 2008, Lainie looked at her son and offered a different response. "Let's leave everything and go on an adventure," she said. "Let's say yes to everything." Miro enthusiastically agreed.

Their planned one-year adventure turned into a more than decade-long journey, and the duo have since become leaders in a growing movement of unschoolers, Worldschoolers, and traveling families. Miro and Lainie organize Project World School, which hosts Worldschooling conferences around the world to bring families together for support and to learn about new and existing educational opportunities.

Through her company, Transformative Mentoring for Teens, Lainie now holds online teen support groups and organizes travel adventures, inspired in part by Miro's own insights and struggles as a teen growing up on the road. She offers courses, group sessions and also one-on-one coaching with teens and men, while also mentoring teens. Her mental health retreats for teenagers include journaling, psychodrama and somatic movement.

Based on her ongoing work, Lainie wrote the book "Seen, Heard & Understood: Parenting & Partnering with Teens for Greater Mental Health." It outlines what she calls the importance of "partnership parenting," which allows parents to support and nurture their children's growth without the need to control and manipulate their kids' personal discovery, she says. Miro, whose own writings are shared on <u>raisingmiro.com</u>, wrote the foreword.

Miro was in his 20s when I interviewed him, and he acknowledged the incredible good fortune and uniqueness of the opportunities his upbringing allowed. It didn't mean there weren't challenges, especially because there aren't many road maps for the lifestyle.

"Nothing looks conventional for Worldschoolers," he said. "So you have to make it up as you go along."

That includes education, making friends, deciding where to live and what you want to be when you grown up. "Aren't these challenges for every young person?"

Adolescence can be difficult whether a teen is traveling or not, so Miro doesn't point to his travels as the sole reason he struggled to find community.

"There's no guarantee that I would have found community or felt any sense of belonging had we not left Los Angeles. So I hesitate to say that that's a unique drawback to this lifestyle. But it definitely is one of them."

"I think we also have this cultural idea of what the ideal social circle looks like. And we fetishize this idea of having this really big social circle. The ideal teenage life is one where in order to be happy, you have to be popular. [You have a] big group of friends, you go to prom... But it's inflated. It's just unrealistic. And the truth of it is that most Americans do not have that many really good friends. They don't even have a couple of close friends, right?"

The mother-son team spent years in Peru in the Andes where Miro formed deep friendships and learned from local indigenous people, while exploring archeological sites.

"If I had studied this particular group of people in some anthropology classroom out of some textbook, would I care as much? Probably not. I might find it interesting on an intellectual level, but that just reduces things to mere interest. In my case, it was personal, it was connection, it was about friendships and relationships. I don't think the educational systems in our culture really lend themselves to that."

In terms of romantic relationships, moving around does have an impact, he admits, but the deeply reflective Miro has thoughts on that, too. He explains that our measure of success about whether a relationship "worked" or was a "success" is very dependent on our expectations.

"We hear a lot, 'oh, it was a successful relationship,' or we have this idea that any relationship that ends was unsuccessful, which is absurd. Just because it comes to an end doesn't mean you didn't grow from it, you didn't learn, you didn't enjoy yourself. Just because something is temporary does not mean that it is a failure. And I think that that is a really huge thing, not just in romantic relationships, but also in friendships and the people you also choose to interact with. In a broader sense it applies to everything."

In traveling communities, you're going to be saying goodbye a lot. "There's nothing wrong with that, Miro says. "People come and go, but it all comes down to the way we judge it and the way that we measure those interactions and relationships."

His deep thinking and wider cultural analysis didn't fit in so well when he tried living in Florida during the pandemic with his then girlfriend. He would try to engage in conversation, but his references to different cultures and world views were seen as arrogance, rather than a rich addition to a given conversation.

"I had to really bite my tongue in a lot of situations because my view of the world is not the same homogenous American view. And if you don't see the world in the same way, people shut down fast. So finding and meeting people is so much harder for me in the US than it is anywhere else in the world."

Miro's life experiences became the groundwork for his current job with a self-directed learning company. He works remotely out of Mexico and still co-leads many of the workshops and conferences with his mother.

Lainie hopes her experiences and vast knowledge can help other teens and young people making their way, and help the parents of those teens as well. Her book invites parents to practice self-inquiry. However well-meaning we parents can be, we're often only as good as our own upbringing and training. Lainie suggests that if we haven't examined the old ideas or fears that we were raised with and that motivate our actions, it can hurt our connection with our children. She encourages all parents to ask themselves whether a given interaction is promoting connection or coercion.

"If you can stop and identify the answer to that question, it can change the outcome of some potentially harmful interactions. The ultimate goal is to make your relationship with your teen stronger."

Which isn't always easy. As many parents know, teens can be particularly good at triggering their parents. If parents haven't begun to look at their own trigger points, then it's more difficult for them to address their teen's mental health, Lainie says. She has particular critiques for the authoritarian model of parenting and the need to control our children. Sure, we want to keep them safe, but she says parents often act out of their own belief systems around what kids "should and shouldn't be doing, and those beliefs aren't necessarily helpful or up to date." Adolescent brain chemistry can present challenges, but not all teens are impulsive and irresponsible. Parents can choose a different belief system or lens through which to view their children; for example, teens are also funny, creative and helpful.

Consider screen time, which at moments might seem like the only thing a young person values. But it likely won't stay that way forever. Lainie says that if screen time is important to your teen right now, then consider: "What's more important, your relationship with your teen or being right and having control?"

Lainie says that Worldschooling helped her become a much better parent.

"I didn't imagine raising a child and being an absentee parent but I didn't have time. I mean, I knew the intellectual way to be present, but I didn't have time to be present."

That all changed when she and Miro began traveling.

"I really stepped outside of a toxic nine-to-five, which was never a nine-to-five lifestyle because I owned a business so I worked all the time. I stepped out of that whole pattern – some people call it the rat race, the hamster wheel. Take that away, and I had time."

Initially, they lived off savings. But when they decided this would be a much longer trip – in fact it might be the beginning of a new life – they had to think creatively about how to make it work. And it wasn't just Lainie making the decisions. Again, she references "partnership parenting."

Miro was only ten when they left the United States, but he was already participating in deep intellectual conversations, Lainie says. So when they decided to extend their travels into more of a lifestyle, he was a partner in making their traveling lifestyle work. Once the decision to extend their trip was made, their mindset had to shift from being on vacation and spending freely to now having a finite amount of money and deciding to travel permanently. That meant that their monthly expenditure in Los Angeles was now their budget for the year. Together they planned their travel and expenses according to this new reality. Miro was given a debit card and advised to take cash and make his spending decisions in accordance with the budget they made together.

Partnership parenting was now part of their family culture – and she suggests every family develop a culture based on shared values.

"One of the ways you can do that is by living without rules. And the way that you live without rules is living according to values."

One of the values that she and Miro shared was deep communication with each other about their internal and external worlds. "So that was normalized in our family as well."

Her book "Seen and Heard" offers tools to help develop and define your own family's values and incorporate them into the family culture. Then decisions are made according to a set of values that has been decided upon using consensus. Not democratic decision making, she warns, because then a family member's voice might not be sufficiently included.

If this process feels a bit uncomfortable, there are several chapters that will help people learn how to identify their emotions, name them, communicate them, and then relate to each other emotionally. She offers examples of important truths that she was never taught as a kid, for example that emotions "are just there to visit us. They're not necessarily truth."

The year 2023 marks the tenth anniversary of the Project World School Family Summits, and each year she has the same conversations with Worldschoolers about developing one's family culture. These conversations always include feelings about fear and discomfort.

"When I speak to Worldschooling groups it's about normalizing the language around comfort zones. What is the comfort zone? What is the stretch zone? And what is the panic zone? And why do we choose to stay in the comfort zone? And what happens to us when that's the only place that we live? What does it feel like to be in the stretch zone?"

She wants people to explore what it means and feels like to be uncomfortable.

"Let's face it, when you're out there traveling, your external world experiences are a reflection of your internal world. There's no getting around it. If you are angry internally, or paranoid or upset, then your experiences in the external world are going to reflect that. So Worldschooling for me, was a really great way for me to really reconcile everything."

You also have to bring joy into the process, she insists. "One of the things that Miro and I brought into our early travels was that we decided we were going to have a theme. Our theme was saying yes to everything, of course within the bounds of safety, but saying yes to everything. That's what we did. We just kept saying yes."

Essential Travel Items

We always travel with our laptops. It serves as entertainment, research and communication; that's super important for both of us.

Additionally, I take a full body pillow, which I've traveled with for 14 years.

We also travel with a stainless steel French press.

Chapter 26

You Have Permission

I have been very aware while writing this book how quickly resources for travelers change. New sites and apps pop up daily, while trusted go-to sources suddenly close down. There is no way to keep up with the range of new and changing resources available to travelers each day. But providing specific resources is not the ultimate goal of this book. Rather it is to answer some of the big questions common to many families who are thinking about traveling and to show you some of the myriad ways that families travel, the incredible resources available, and where to begin to research more.

This book gives you permission.

I wrote it to answer common questions but also to encourage people who felt like these experiences were out of reach. I wanted readers to see themselves in these pages, and to feel empowered to look further. This book is only a first step, but it might just be your biggest step of all. Giving yourself permission is the key to opening a door to your new future. Take it. You have permission to take your kids out of school. You have permission to educate your children in a way that better suits your family and your lifestyle. You have permission to ask for a new way of working or to change careers if it makes you and your family happier and healthier. You have permission to travel. Whatever your family size and makeup, you have permission.

We are here for you. We are a community of traveling families with so much knowledge, so many suggestions, resources, and wonderful experiences to share. We are eager to continue building this community of people who want to live differently, and we look forward to meeting you on the road. Hope to see you soon!

A camel ride in Cairo, Egypt.
Suddenly my little boy is bigger than me.

Epilogue

When my son was fifteen we organized a group trip with two other Worldschooling families to Athens, Greece. There were five kids in total, including a solo 16-year-old traveler who heard of this meet-up and asked to join. A friend of mine who was new to Worldschooling, and world travel with kids in general, joined as well. One night the kids all participated in an escape room adventure in downtown Athens. The parents chose to have a calm dinner and after the meal gathered at one of the families' Airbnb for a drink. As it neared midnight and still no word from the kids, my new-to-Worldschooling friend became anxious. As he clearly pointed out, we had forgotten to give the kids a curfew and few had working phones (so the Life360 app I always used to track Aiden's whereabouts wasn't working either). The Worldschooling families were initially unmoved. The kids were in a group, knew the rules to stay together and watch out for one another, and since the youngest was only ten, they wouldn't be sneaking into any late-night discoteques. But my friend's fear was contagious. What if the kids decided to stay out all night? They didn't have a curfew, after all. What if they were trying to call us and simply couldn't?

Frustration more than panic set in, and by 1am we organized a search party. We set out in different directions, making sure to walk any street that might lead them home. My friend and I walked the half hour to the escape room building – long closed – before getting a text that the group had been intercepted, Gelato in hands, walking home. "Of course we weren't going to stay out too late, mom. Julie is only 10," Aiden explained to me later, completely unaware that his meeting up with search party member Jim was not coincidental.

I'm glad we found them quickly and it was a good reminder to set curfews and make sure phones are working. But we also trusted that these kids had a strong street sense about them. Most had been traveling all their lives. They knew how to ask for directions, navigate a bus and metro map, and stay together to best avoid trouble. When they were "found" they had been discussing an organized (parent-free) Worldschooling trip to Patagonia later that year. They would all apply, they decided. They compared their language skills and decided Aiden spoke the best Spanish. (Aiden did apply and despite being a year under the required age, convinced the program director to let him join. The month-long trip would be his first time away from home by himself).

We left each other and returned to our respective corners of the world – including Eastern Europe, Canada, Indiana and New Mexico – but that event stayed with me. It was a reminder of the intelligence, confidence and practical skills that travel instills in our kids. I love that my son is connected with other Worldschoolers and will soon begin his own adventures. His worldliness and confidence, language ability and knowledge of other countries, will open doors and build bridges. I am optimistic these skills will expand his employment opportunities and the span of his job search to include any country he chooses. Plus, he's had a lot of fun.

My desire is that his experiences have made the basis for a rich and beautiful life full of stories, wonderful people and a variety of perspectives on how different countries and political systems work. I hope it makes him grateful for the opportunities and good fortune he has had, and that one day he'll tell stories to his own children about the things he learned and saw, and how he wants similar experiences for them. Because travel is a teacher — and a gift — like none other.

Alicia Cardenas

This book is for Alicia Cardenas and all the parents of the world who want to create a more safe, creative, and extraordinary life for their children. In the face of a thousand messages telling us how to live and how education should look, there are those who know there is another way. Whether it's bucking the Euro-centric, colonialist model for a truer concept of culture and

self, or simply feeling frustrated with your child's cur-
rent school, this is for you. You are the revolutionaries
who know that life can be an exceptionally rich and
wonderful adventure if you just open your eyes and
heart to a new path.

On December 27, 2021, Alicia, a mother, mentor, tat-
too artist, body piercer, and former President of the
Association of Professional Piercers was shot and
killed in her studio in Denver, Colorado. She leaves
behind a daughter and a community that loved her
fiercely.

I have kept this specific interview in her own words to
best preserve this beautiful personality and voice. She
is deeply missed.

I'm from Colorado, but my family is from the North
American Indians of Taos Pueblo. We're also *Meshika*
[Aztec people who spoke Nahuatl language], which is
from the center of Mexico. I identify as a Native person
from the north and from the south, but I was raised in
Denver, Colorado. My partner is from Ireland. We have
an eight-year-old "Two Spirit" daughter, Xochitl, who's
here with us for this Worldschooling summit. We travel throughout Mexico, but we're here specifically in

Guanajuato for the summit. We just got back from Ireland last month, and we pretty much travel about six months out of the year.

We have a home base in the US where I've had a business for 25 years. Because of that business, I'm able to travel and go back and work as needed. I'm an artist and I can also work pretty much anywhere that I go. I'll often do guest spots or set up a gig ahead of time, so I will travel to a place where I'll be able to work and then explore.

I own a tattoo and body piercing studio in Colorado, I have for a long time. So I can basically make appointments to go work at other studios all over the world. Also, I seek out opportunities to paint because I do mural work. If I have an opportunity to paint somewhere, then that's a good opportunity to pick up and take everybody to a place and paint there. Either it's tattooing or painting, and it's been great. I now have friends all over the world from previous travels, and that allows me to make a living and continue to travel.

I was led to Worldschooling, which is a new concept for us. We've been basing our schooling off a more traditional Native approach to schooling a child, which is that our child has never been away from me. We had a home birth, we've done all the educating in home, and my kid is our main focus. Everything is based around what works for her, and traveling really works for her. She loves to explore, she gets bored easily, she does not sit in a classroom. That's not part of her thing. She's an artist so everything's interpreted through art, and song, music, and dance. That's kind of how we got inspired to do as much traveling as possible.

All our travel is challenging. Integrating into other cultures is always challenging. Integrating the European culture with my more Native perspective has been challenging. Even though my partner is very aligned with me, he still comes from a predominantly Euro centric sort of mentality, and we are fully not that. So constantly having challenges, but not nearly as many as when we tried to put Xochitl into a classroom setting. Way more challenges there, way more.

The benefits [we've gained from travel] is a very strong, culturally aware, comfortable, bright, intuitive, healing, awesome, energetic, strong, independent child who has constantly challenged me, which is what I've taught her to do. [laughs]

We always go towards where it's best for my child, because we always have my kid with us. Mexico is really kid friendly, kid appreciative, kid centered. This is a great place to be. Honestly, we try to adapt wherever we are. So there have been places where I definitely don't let her wander as freely. Part of this schooling is about having them learn to navigate what is safe and what isn't safe, and being able to communicate in other languages is necessary for your safety. That's part of the curriculum as well: places that are friendly or unfriendly where she needs to be closer to me or where she can be running a little bit more freely. I would say Mexico is a great spot for that, pretty much anything in Latin America, or South America is very kid oriented and friendly.

I found that Europe is not so good with that. That's also a reflection of the culture: Kids are to be seen, not heard. Kids are not as respected. They're not as incorporated. There's a time and place for kids. It's a different culture. If anything, that's the cultural element that comes creeping in on my relationship that is very challenging, because my partner is having to learn how to respect children differently than how he was taught.

I'm still working through my indoctrination around schooling and my decolonization around what it takes to be a successful human on this planet. I was raised in a very traditional Catholic home where, as a Chicana, it was prioritized that you become as much an academic, as you can get. I was only the second generation to make it through college so it was a big focus to be the smartest, brightest student in school.

Having gone through all that, really having been pushed academically through my life, what I'm grateful for, and humbled by, is landing as an artist. I'm living a very blissed out, happy life, not doing anything that I was trained to do. In my business I had to do a lot of mathematics initially. Everything that I don't like to do, I am now happily delegating to others, and I'm able to freely move as an artist. I found my happiness in that sort of hand work, creating with your hands, as opposed to using your mind for everything, or your mind solely.

So, yeah, I'm decolonizing around that and figuring out what's important, which is a happy, well-rounded child who is comfortable in multiple cultures and can speak multiple languages. I still let some of that worry creep in just like anybody else. My daughter is sort of that duality, there's two to three hours every morning of some focused studies, starting with art and ending with art, but in the middle is cursive and writing and reading and mathematics, and then ending with a whole afternoon of unschooling. She doesn't like the word unschooling; she prefers to call it nature schooling, because we are spending a lot of time outdoors. We're doing a lot of camping, fire building, spiritual work, studying stones and animals.

I think I'm getting more loose about what our morning activities entail, but she is learning her mathematics and her writing and reading and cursive writing in the morning. We're still breaking it up half and half, as I need a little structure to move through my own curriculum. It helps us get focused for the rest of the day of play and museum visiting, and that type of stuff.

I think it's interesting that everybody here [at the Worldschooling conference] is going back to original design that happened throughout the history of indigenous people, and acting like it's some new concept [laughs]. I think it's important for us to understand what has happened in humanity in the past in order to move forward. My advice would be to go back to basics, and find out who your kid is, and then go forward from there. Because many people go through society allowing other people to raise their children. I was not okay spending six to eight hours away and having my kid in the hands of somebody who I did not know, who wasn't a part of my family, and who I didn't have an understanding of their philosophy or their connection to this planet.

I think that people need to go back into their own family histories and see what their great, great grandparents did, and figure out what works for them and incorporate that moving forward. A lot of times there was already homeschooling, Worldschooling, nature schooling, hands-on craftsmen, vocational schooling happening within family units prior to being indoctrinated by this kind of modern society that would work well and also serve the soul of the family, not just the production of the family. Figuring out who your kid is can sometimes be really painful, because you're learning all the bad stuff first, like, what doesn't work for them, as opposed to focusing on what does work.

As a culture we've been indoctrinated to problem solve the problems before the good stuff. I would say go back to what works and you exploit that as much as humanly possible. Then deprioritize the stuff that doesn't work and move freely through it back to the stuff that does work. Be patient and be loving and forgiving of yourself. Because this culture also teaches us that we have to lash ourselves or self-flog when we don't do things right, or when things don't go the way that we want. Once you let go of the reins, you'll be pleasantly surprised at what comes forward from there, and you can do it competently. There's a lot of people competently leading our children into darkness. So why not competently lead your child into the family soul and the lightness that comes with surrendering to the natural design of your child?

What would I do differently? I'm still so much in the thick of it with the eight-year-old that I would say, I probably would have had more children maybe? No, I'm good. [laughter]

Differently? I don't know, I don't live in a world of regret. My philosophy is even the bad stuff, to just be rolling with it and learning from it. We all wish that with certain little things we had maybe dealt in that moment differently. I guess I wish I had listened to my child sooner about certain things. You have that guilt and that feeling of 'Oh, I can't let them be in charge of everything. I have to sometimes implement my wants, desires and needs upon them.' But turns out she was right about everything that has not worked out.

I feel like when I rooted myself as a parent in trying to be respectful of who my child was, I still hadn't had my ears completely open to who she was. It took a few years of having her prove me wrong. Time and time again. I was like, Well wait, she's a really smart person who I should listen to. Listening not to what is being said, but what is being told, what is being communicated. Maybe not in all these words, but in actions. So having that sort of connection with her.

Also, I think living off of the earth, off grid living like we're doing now in Denver is something that I wish I had been doing all along. It would be nice to have never even introduced iPads to the scenario, but there are still very long plane rides involved with this way of life. Sometimes you have to use your modern version of self in order to get through some of those more difficult moments.

People think that in order to travel, you have to have a lot of money. That's a misnomer. I think sometimes it's just a lack of creativity and lack of good planning. I encourage people, even if they feel like this is a very specific group that can handle or do this, it's not. You can actually save money by traveling. I spend more money in Denver than I do traveling. So if you just cut out some of those ridiculous habits, like having sushi every week, you can build up a very good base of money to be able to take some pretty extravagant feeling trips.

Also being fearless about cooking off of an open fire or off of a camp stove. We bring camp stoves with us so we can afford to be there longer and have more food available to us, instead of eating out every day.

Essential Travel Items

We can't get enough of computer research. That's such an important part of what we do to figure out where we want to go or what we want to do. Computers are a pretty important part of all that.

The iPad is kind of our default; you can get a lot of good programs, educational programs, too. If Xochitl masters something we get it off the iPad and we get something new on. She feels very accomplished when she's wiped out her iPad, and

---

we've got all new things on the horizon. iPads are really good, playing card games with your family is really good. Basically, using the same games throughout all the different cultures, like word games, so that you can learn the language.

I would say no matter how much you travel, you should have sacred things that you carry with yourself, because there's going to be times that are really uncomfortable. If you have incense or a candle or something that your family identifies no matter where you are, those types of things can help ground a family: Music or smells or feelings or songs that can be carried with you always, that are going to create that instantaneous comfort in a difficult situation. You've just been on a 12-hour flight, you're on a taxi ride in a foreign country in the middle of the night, and now your kid has to go to the bathroom? It's pretty important to have a song that's going to hold on for five more minutes until you can get to the bathroom. Or having taught my kid to pee and poop on the earth has been a really valuable asset in those moments. So, you know, sometimes it's really complex, and sometimes it's really easy.

Padar Island. Komodo, Indonesia

"Tell me, what is it you plan to do with your one wild and precious life?"

-Mary Oliver

INDEX

Below is a list of resources mentioned in this book by me and other travelers. These are items that have made our travels easier and more comfortable. If you buy directly from the links provided (in the ebook version), I will get a small commission. In other cases, the links are purely informational to help you access the sites that travelers have used and learned from.

Lori Greene
Yeti coolers and wine glasses
Phone charger/battery

Jacqui and Daniel New
Kobo eReader

Alicia E.
Power strip surge protector

Paul Carlino and Rebecca Eichler
Power strip surge protector
Maps.me
ioverlander.com
Boondockerswelcome.com

Campendium.com

Outdoorsy.com

Allison Sherman

Professor, Author, Podcaster and motivational speaker Brené Brown speaks on leadership, vulnerability and shame. She is hysterically funny and deep. Whatever self-improvement and growth is necessary for your next step, make sure Brené Brown is included.

The Power of Vulnerability

This is the 2010 TED talk that put Brown on the map.

Chapter 7 - Build Your Community

adventuringatoz.com

Worldschoolingcentral.com by Karen King (she also hosts worldschoolingdirectory.com)

WeAreWorldschoolers.org

Worldtravelfamily.com

Worldschoolerexchange.com

Worldschoolinghub.com

Worldschoolpopuphub.com

ProjectWorldschool.com

Raisingmiro.com

Thewanderingdaughter.com

Pearceonearth.com

Homealongtheway.com

Enlightenedglobetrekker.com
Dreamtimetraveler.com
Arightsizedlife.com
Boundless.life
Thetravellingblizzards.com
Jenn Miller @JennLately
PanAmerican Travelers Association on Facebook

Karen and Cameron King
10-port USB Hub
Google Nest mini
Trustedhousesitters.com

Chapter 8
NomadList.com
Numbeo.com
Happy Heart Travel Facebook page

Chapter 10
Central America-4 Border Control Agreement
schengenvisainfo.com
Nolo.com
RocketLawyer.com

Chapter 11
Airbnb.com
VRBO.com

Hostelworld.com

Cards Against Humanity

PeopleLikeUs.world

Craigslist.com

Boundless.life

Trustedhousesitters.com

Homeexchange.com

Lovehomeswap.com

Wwoof.net

Workaway.info

Peacecorps.gov

Volunteerforever.com

GoEco.org

ViaVolunteers.com

Kibbutzvolunteer.com

Jesica Sweedler DeHart

iPad

maps.me

OverDrive

LEGOs

Electric Shaver

Neutrogena 70 SPF sunscreen

Compression Packing Cubes

Jay Shapiro

Tripit.com

Lydia Bradbury
Daddy Dolls
Third Culture Kids: **Growing Up Among Worlds**

Chapter 16 - Schooling on the Road
Galileoxp.com
KhanAcademy.org
Udemy.com
Adam Ruins Everything/truTV.com
ScienceNews.org
Vlogbrothers on Youtube
iCivics.org
Masterclass.com
YouTube.com
Unschooling/hackschooling

@Omniseducation
Outschool.com
iTunes U
Coursera.org
Lynda.com
Brightstorm.com
CodeAcademy.com
OpenCulture.com

For younger kids there is <u>FactMonster</u>, <u>CoolMath Games</u>, <u>PBS Kids</u> (Jet Go! And Kratt Brothers were favorites). <u>Thinkrolls Play & Code</u>, <u>Science 360</u>.

For language learning there is <u>Duolingo</u>, <u>Yabla</u>, or <u>Babbel</u>.

Music: <u>Yousician</u> and <u>Pianu</u>

Jennifer Sutherland
@Omniseducation

Chapter 17 - Single Parent or Solo Travel
<u>Carbon Monoxide Detector</u>
<u>Life360.com</u> – The #1 Family safety and location sharing app

Chapter 18 – Healthcare on the Road
Medicines from my PERSONAL travel bag (please consult your physician for a medical kit that is best for your family): <u>Colloidal Silver</u>, <u>Band Aids</u>, <u>tweezers</u>, <u>Neosporin</u>, antibiotics, <u>Benadryl</u>, <u>children's Tylenol</u>, <u>Aspirin</u>, lots of <u>Vitamin C</u>, a good <u>thermometer</u>, <u>gauze and bandages</u>. <u>Rescue Remedy</u> drops or candies and a good multi vitamin and immune booster. For airplanes: <u>calm forté</u>, a homeopathic sleep aid. Other suggestions include carrying <u>eyedrops</u>; <u>Dramamine</u>, particularly if

one is prone to motion sickness; <u>Tums</u> for minor stomach upset; <u>Liquid Band-Aides</u>, <u>Anti flu packets</u>, and <u>Oscillococcinum</u>, a homeopathic remedy for influenza, to be taken immediately upon the first symptom.

Chapter 19 - Travel Insurance
<u>SevenCorners.com</u>
<u>Allianze.com</u>
<u>TravelInsurance.com</u>
<u>RoamRight.com</u>
<u>WorldNomads.com</u>
<u>TrawickInternational.com</u>

CHAPTER 20 - Financing Your Travel/Jobs on the Road
<u>Nomadlist.com</u>
<u>Numbeo.com</u>
<u>InterNations</u>
Geoarbitrage
<u>The Remote Nomad</u>
<u>Working Nomads</u>
<u>The 4 Hour Work Week</u> by Tim Ferriss
<u>Die With Zero</u>; Getting all you can from your Money and Your Life by Bill Perkins
<u>Mr. Money Mustache</u>
<u>Making Sense of Cents</u>

Bigger Pockets

ChooseFi.com

Afford Anything by Paula Pant

Rich Dad Poor Dad

Flexjobs

Indeed

Remotewoman.com

schwab.com

fi.google.com

Scottscheapflights.com

Skyscanner.com

Expedia.com

Orbitz.com

Hopper.com

Groupon.com

Volaris.com

Easyjet.com

Eurail.com

seat61.com

Eurovelo.com

Aironwardticket.com

Vacationstogo.com

Turo.com

Getaround.com

Uber.com

Lyft.com

Grab.com

BlablaCar.com

Outdoorsy.com

Rvezy.com

Autodriveaway.com

Parsinc.com

Credit Card Points

Thepointsguy.com

@Milesmom

Familiesflyfree.com

AwardWallet.com

Points.com

Cashbackmonitor.com

To Access Money Abroad: schwab.com

Tracey Tullis

Headlamps with extra battery pack

Scrubba wash bags

Chapter 21 - Some Necessities for Remote Working

WiFi

GoogleFi

Travelwifi.com

Starlink.com

SpaceX.com

Chanel Morales

Skyscanner.com

Airbnb.com

Workaway.info

Homestay.com

Her Masterclass on earning $5k a month

Scrubba Washbags

Laptop lift

iPhone tripod

Chanel Morales coaching – thedreamclub.co.uk

Chapter 22 - Travel Smarter

Stainless steel camping cutlery

Reusable plastic and bamboo sets

Diva Cup or Mooncup.co.uk

Thinx Period Underwear

Baggus

Bamboo toothbrush

Kindle Fire Tablet

Clint Bush and Astrid Vinje

Dry Erase Sheets

Wireless internet booster

Laptop Lift
External Keyboard
Mouse
Ipad
Clubhouse App
Notion.so
Roku extra or ultra
Carbon Monoxide Detector
SCOOPS card game

Chapter 23 – Relationships
Hellorelish.com
Gottman's Eight Dates

Sandra Odems
GPS land/air/sea tracker or Garmin Satellite Communicator

Lainie Liberti and Miro Siegel
raisingmiro.com
Project World School
ProjectWorldSchool.com

Alicia Cardenas
iPad

A few popular hubs popular with remote workers and families:

San Miguel de Allende, Guanajuato, Playa del Carmen and Puerto Vallarta, Mexico; Chiang Mai, Thailand; Bali, Indonesia; Andalucia, Spain; Santo Domingo, Dominican Republic

Some organized communities around the world:

-Anahataworldschoolingcommunity.com is a popular location for families in southern Mexico. They run three-month programs year-round.

-Worldschoohubandalucia.com for Worldschoolers in Spain.

-Stagingjourneys.com which works to build community through travel, learning and theater

-Unschooladventures.com run by Blake Boles, offers big adventures for self-directed teens. Aiden joined his month-long trip to Patagonia and loved it.

-Projectworldschool.com run by Lainie Liberti, offers Worldschooling conferences around the world, as well as mental health programs for traveling teens.

Magazines: International Living magazine offers stories primarily for people wishing to retire overseas.

Many adventures are close to home.
Camping is a great way to get your kids out of doors.

INDEX

Here is a list of favorite board games for families on the Go.

Apples to Apples
Alhambra
Banangrams
Bang
Barenpark
Battleship
Blockus
Bug Bingo
Cacao: Chocolatl
Carcassonne
Cashflow for Kids
Chess
Dragonwood
Evolution: The Beginning
Exploding Kittens
Fluxx
Forbidden Island
Geography Bingo
Ice Cool
Ingenious
Dixit
Doodle Dice
Farkle

Hanabi

Killer Bunnies

King of Tokyo

Ligretto

Loonacy

Machi Koro

Make n' Break

Mancala

Monopoly

Munchkin

Phase Ten

Pass The Pigs

Munchkin

Pirate Fluxx

Qwirkle

RACKO

Ravensburger Labyrinth

Risk

Rory's Story Cubes – Voyages

Rush Hour

Scrabble

Scoops (created by a Worldschooling family!)

Skull

Scotland Yard

Sequence

SET (cards, not a mobile)

Settlers of Catan! And Catan junior

Skip-Bo

Sleeping Queens

Smallworld

Splendor

Starving Artists

Sushi Go!

S'quarrels: A Game of Absolute Nuts

10 days in Asia (they have other continents as well)

Take Off

Takenono

Ticket to RIDE

Tokaido

Upwords

Wildcraft

Word on the Street Jr.

Tsuro

Uno

ABOUT THE AUTHOR

Zélie Pollon is an award-winning journalist who spent decades working for Reuters, The Dallas Morning News, People magazine and other publications, covering New Mexico and such epic historical events as the Iraq war. She traveled throughout the Southwest telling stories of people, the environment, and political crises.

A dual citizen of France and America she grew up traveling and eventually chose to complete her graduate work in Europe. She was a Rotary International Peace Fellow in England, and completed her

Master's thesis in Cambodia, documenting survivors of the Khmer Rouge. After years of print journalism, she moved to radio and served as news director for two community radio stations in New Mexico.

While covering the war in Iraq she fell in love with her translator and three years later, after helping this man escape the country, was blessed with a beautiful son. By the age of five her son already had more passport stamps than most American adults. Zélie is currently – and always – planning her next adventure.